Thriving as a Superintendent

How to Recognize and Survive an Unanticipated Departure

Thomas F. Evert and Amy E. Van Deuren

Published in Partnership with the
American Association of School Administrators

ROWMAN & LITTLEFIELD EDUCATION

A division of
ROWMAN & LITTLEFIELD PUBLISHERS, INC.
Lanham • New York • Toronto • Plymouth, UK

Published in partnership with the American Association of School Administrators

Published by Rowman & Littlefield Education
A division of Rowman & Littlefield Publishers, Inc.
A wholly owned subsidiary of The Rowman & Littlefield Publishing Group, Inc.
4501 Forbes Boulevard, Suite 200, Lanham, Maryland 20706
www.rowman.com

10 Thornbury Road, Plymouth PL6 7PP, United Kingdom

Copyright © 2013 by Thomas F. Evert and Amy E. Van Deuren

All rights reserved. No part of this book may be reproduced in any form or by any electronic or mechanical means, including information storage and retrieval systems, without written permission from the publisher, except by a reviewer who may quote passages in a review.

British Library Cataloguing in Publication Information Available

Library of Congress Cataloging-in-Publication Data Available

ISBN 978-1-4758-0301-3 (cloth) — ISBN 978-1-4758-0302-0 (pbk.)
ISBN 978-1-4758-0303-7 (electronic)

Table of Contents

Acknowledgments		vii
1	Overview and Context	1
2	The Story of Roberta K.	11
3	The Story of Richard B.	25
4	The Story of Randy J.	43
5	Interview Process, Demographics, and Development of Frameworks	61
6	Lessons Learned Using the Superintendent Experience and Unanticipated Departure Frameworks	79
Appendix 1		109
Appendix 2		111
Appendix 3		115
References		119
About the Authors		121

Acknowledgments

This book is dedicated to the twenty-two superintendents who agreed to be interviewed and who provided their insights into the dynamics of unanticipated departures. They have shared invaluable advice, both cognitive and affective in nature.

We would both like to acknowledge and thank Diane Wesner for her expertise and speed in turning around drafts and other materials in record time, and most importantly, for her insight, experience, and expertise "behind the scenes" in all things related to school district central office happenings. Diane possesses a unique gift for doing each job right and asking the right questions at the right times. Thank you.

Each of us also has individual people we would like to recognize.

Amy:

I would like to recognize my father, Marty, whose inspirational career as a high school English teacher and basketball and track coach fostered and nurtured my own career in education, and my mother, Lynn, whose faith, support, and pragmatic yet optimistic outlook has made all the difference in the world between success and failure. Last but certainly not least, I would like to thank my daughter, Isabelle, who is my inspiration for the future and my most precious gift.

Tom:

I would like to thank my wife, retired superintendent Bette Lang, for her support and for allowing us the time it took to focus on this effort, not to mention her vital role in offering just the right advice and mediation during critical junctures. I would also like to acknowledge my daughter Kris, son-in-law Jerry, son Jeff, and daughter-in-law Julie, all of whom are deeply involved in public education as teachers and parents. Finally, I would like to acknowledge their children, Erik, Noah, Caleb, and Leo, who inspire and motivate me to continue in my own personal journey in public education.

Chapter One

Overview and Context

Superintendents are trained to solve problems. They anticipate problems, deal with difficult and challenging situations, and build coalitions to (hopefully) make positive strides in their districts for students, staff, and the community. However, when problems arise that deal directly with their own effectiveness as a leader and ability to lead, a superintendent's problem-solving abilities may not be up to the task. There is great variability among superintendents as to how they interpret and react to district turmoil, particularly as it relates to their own positions and futures. In short, most superintendents have had no training and no experience with an unanticipated departure from the superintendency or the departure process until they actually go through it.

Eadie (2003, 2005, 2012) has written extensively about the importance of school board governance and board/superintendent relationships. He states that "the school board—superintendent working relationship is notoriously fragile, and is very likely to erode if not meticulously managed—witness the all-too-frequent ugly and public breakups" (2012, p. 38). These ugly and public breakups are the stuff of unanticipated departures.

Eadie's comments underlie the fact that enough turmoil and unrest in a district can ultimately cripple a superintendent's ability to effectively lead. Often, turmoil is exacerbated by the chaos that develops as more stakeholders become involved in the turmoil. When the issue is the effectiveness of the superintendent, he or she must consider whether to stay and fight through the issue or whether it is time to consider leaving the position.

An unanticipated superintendent departure can happen in many different ways and may be initiated by the board, the superintendent, or both. These include: (1) issues with the board, internal audiences, external publics, and the media (alone or in combination); (2) disagreement on short-term or long-term goals that has created unrest; and (3) the superintendent spending political capital on small items that add up to big resentment over time ("rocks in your pockets").

ISSUES WITH THE BOARD, INTERNAL AUDIENCES, EXTERNAL PUBLICS, AND THE MEDIA

The degree to which the board and superintendent work together effectively covers a wide spectrum. On the positive end of the spectrum, the board and superintendent are in perfect harmony on how to plan for and address the many facets of school leadership and school management issues. On the negative end of the spectrum, the board members are constantly at odds with the superintendent (and usually among themselves), and little is done to move the district forward in any meaningful way (Walser, 2009). When the board and superintendent are functioning at the negative end of the spectrum, it can be very challenging indeed for a superintendent to continue working in the district through completion of his or her contract.

A superintendent's working relationship with internal audiences is critical to his or her success. Internal audiences, whether or not they are union-represented, are the source of many issues that a superintendent must address. Disciplinary concerns, remediation, and legal issues are typically ongoing and always carry some risk that they may spin out of control and affect the superintendent's ability to lead effectively in his or her position. Staff resentment and unrest, whether to a small or large degree, can also affect the ability of a superintendent to serve out his or her contract.

External publics can also affect a superintendent's ability to effectively serve out a contract. Relationships with local businesses, civic organizations, parent groups, and the media are critical to both promoting current good work and future programs. In addition, these external audiences and the media are important factors in determining how much attention an issue will receive in the community.

DISAGREEMENT ON SHORT-TERM OR LONG-TERM GOALS

When the board and the superintendent (and/or administration and staff) do not agree on short-term or long-term goals, it can spell disaster for the superintendent. This scenario is most likely to happen after a superintendent has been in the district for some time; after all, most boards try to hire a superintendent whose goals and priorities align with their own. However, as time goes on, things change. New board members are elected and districts face new problems and mandates, such as significantly decreased budgets and more pressure for higher test scores.

At some point, it can become apparent that the board's (and perhaps the community's) priorities are no longer in alignment with what the superintendent was hired to do. The board may eventually demand a change in leadership, or the superintendent may decide that he or she can no longer do what the board is asking.

SPENDING POLITICAL CAPITAL

Superintendents must make choices about what to support and advocate for and what to leave alone for another day. Depending on the issue, the level of controversy, and the commitment of the superintendent to achieve a desired outcome, the superintendent may end up spending personal political capital in addressing the issue. Over time, this expenditure of political capital (whether with the board, internal audiences, or the community) can result in weakened effectiveness as a leader, a phenomenon sometimes referred to as "rocks in your pockets" (Patterson, 2000).

For example, a superintendent may support a new initiative, thinking that the community climate is right for such action. When the pushback on the initiative is greater than originally anticipated, the superintendent must decide whether to move forward with the initiative or put it on the back burner. If the superintendent decides to move forward, one of the things he or she must reassess is the amount of personal and political capital that might be spent getting the initiative passed, and he or she needs to understand that the likelihood it will result in another rock or two in his or her pocket is very high.

Sometimes, a superintendent knows that an issue will require political capital in order to reach a satisfactory resolution. Other times, an issue requires using unanticipated political capital. The reality is that most district leaders will experience the detrimental effects of spent political capital during their superintendencies, regardless of how it is accumulated. These "rocks in your pockets" (see chapter 2) can accumulate over time until the superintendent is no longer seen as a good fit with the district, which can result in an unanticipated departure.

One professor who teaches future superintendents told students that "rocks in your pockets" would accumulate at the rate of 20 percent per year until, after five years, they would no longer be able to move. This is a metaphor both humorous and frightening, and perhaps somewhat exaggerated, but it certainly contains at least a dose of reality. It articulates an important point: Smaller issues can add up to significant political capital over time.

This book explores unanticipated departures from the superintendency as a common enough occurrence that every superintendent should be aware of its possibility. The reality is that unanticipated departures can occur to any superintendent at any time, regardless of ability or experience. Drawing from the experiences of twenty-two superintendents who have been through unanticipated departures offers readers a unique opportunity to gain insight into the totality of the departure process. The material in this book covers superintendents' experiences regarding events leading up to the departure, when the superintendents realized it was time to leave the position, how they went about actually leaving, and how they recovered and learned from the experience afterward.

In addition to the experiences of superintendents who have lived through the unanticipated departure experience, this book includes three detailed scenarios for study and discussion. Two scenarios depict superintendents in various stages in their careers who must decide whether they should leave before the end of their contracted tenure. The third superintendent has already experienced an unanticipated departure and is reflecting on the experience in his new superintendent role while preparing to teach a university-level course on educational leadership. The scenarios include questions for reflection and discussion, and a review of pertinent, relevant books and articles that can serve as a basis for further exploration and research on unanticipated departures.

This book covers a wide range of superintendent experiences, including beginning, mid-career, and long-term superintendents. We learned that each experience level (number of years of service as a superintendent) carries its own unique challenges and considerations. The stories and information in this book represent many facets of the superintendency, and it is our intention that there is something that will resonate with all readers, whether they are aspiring to be superintendents, are serving as new superintendents, or are seasoned veterans in the superintendency.

WHY IS SUPERINTENDENT UNANTICIPATED DEPARTURE IMPORTANT?

The high rate of turnover in the superintendency is well documented, with recent estimated tenure averages ranging from 3 to 5.6 years (Domenech, 2011; Sutton & Job, 2008). Regardless of the actual number, there is general agreement that turnover occurs more frequently than is optimal (Marzano, Waters, & McNulty 2009; Pascopella, 2011). American Association of School Administrators (AASA) executive director Dan Domenech, speaking at the 2011 Wisconsin Association of School District Administrators (WASDA) fall conference, stated that superintendents are the education field's "migrant workers." The high rate of superintendent turnover alone warrants a closer look at superintendent departures.

There are other factors that contribute to making the study of unanticipated superintendent departures timely and necessary. In many parts of the country, there are fewer qualified candidates available and more career exits (Keane & Moore, 2001; Kowalski, McCord, Peterson, Young, & Ellerson, 2011). Current political unrest and change in education, evidenced strongly in Ohio, Indiana, and Wisconsin, add to the tensions and uncertainty faced in many districts as budgets tighten and long-held protocols and systems (such as collective bargaining for teachers) are being questioned and changed (Underwood, 2011). Finally, research is more opinion-based than fact-based regarding why boards hire and fire superintendents (Mathews, Floyd, Ilg, & Rohn, 2002), creating additional uncertainty and tension for district leaders.

Most superintendents go into their positions with at least some awareness of these factors surrounding the superintendency but may not immediately recognize when issues and problems, which are inherent in the position, go from being "fixable" to "unfixable." An important aspect of a "successful" unanticipated departure is recognizing the warning signs of the unfixable and moving forward in a way that causes minimal damage to the district and to the career that the superintendent has worked so hard to establish. It is critical that superintendents are as prepared as possible in the event that an unanticipated departure becomes imminent.

That is not to say that a superintendent should consider leaving at the first sign of trouble—far from it. Superintendents as a rule are simply not wired that way. They are individuals trained to resolve conflict and build coalitions in order to improve student learning in the districts that they serve. Dealing with conflict and addressing difficult issues are part and parcel of the position. However, superintendents also need the capacity to step back and assess the bigger picture in terms of their roles in moving the district forward.

Perhaps gaining more insight into unanticipated superintendent departures may help some superintendents avoid what seems inevitable. However, *avoiding the departure is not the purpose of this book*; rather, it is to recognize and successfully negotiate the waters of an unanticipated departure should it occur. If an unanticipated departure cannot be avoided, being prepared and demonstrating exemplary leadership throughout the process will protect both the district and the superintendent so that life can move forward for both in a positive manner.

The relationship between the superintendent and district (particularly the board) is often analogized as a "marriage" with good reason, partly because of the manner in which these relationships are entered into and dissolved (Eadie, 2009). In short, we contend that there are some "right" and "wrong" ways to go about an unanticipated departure, and the reality is that a person can only control his or her own behavior, not the behavior of those around him or her.

This book provides practical advice from the superintendents interviewed regarding what they did well and what they wish they had done differently during the departure process. This advice is beneficial for superintendents and aspiring superintendents at any point in their careers, whether or not they are currently experiencing difficulty that may lead to an unanticipated departure. In short, the stories and advice from those superintendents who have undergone unanticipated departures are important for what they can offer to help all superintendents be more effective in their roles as educational leaders.

STATE AND NATIONAL CONTEXTS ARE STILL IMPORTANT

It is no wonder that superintendents and school boards are sometimes at odds in 2012. Since the 1980s, public schools have received ever-increasing attention and scrutiny. In *A Nation at Risk* (1983), the authors engaged in new levels of criticism about the quality of education offered in America's public schools and made specific recommendations for improvement. "The report propelled a move from measuring school quality by resources received and onto a plane where performance is judged on outcomes students achieve" (Guthrie & Springer, 2004). This report fueled the increase of federal government involvement in education, and education reform continued throughout the 1990s.

The 1990s were marked by increased pressure on public schools to stress curriculum standards, student achievement, and standardized testing. These trends were reflected in the 1994 reauthorization of the Elementary and Secondary Education Act (ESEA) and the Improving America's Schools Act (IASA), which were marked by adding standards for assessment to provide accountability for student achievement.

This push for accountability was a result of national politicians—such as Bill Clinton, George W. Bush, and Ted Kennedy—calling for more federal involvement in education and higher student achievement throughout the nation as reflected in standardized test scores. However, it was not until the passage of NCLB in 2001 that accountability for student achievement through standardized testing became a full-scale reality.

A new twist has been added to federal funding with the introduction of Race to the Top funds, introduced in 2009 as part of the American Recovery and Reinvestment Act. This federal legislation resulted in many states changing state legislation and policies to become competitive for the federal funds and also accelerated the push toward common core standards, a critical component for Race to the Top funding.

Currently, other pressures are being placed on superintendents and school boards as well. Many states are cutting funding to education, while demands for student achievement and staff accountability at all levels continue to increase. Demands for increased technological capacity require updates and installations to district infrastructures. Many districts are experiencing increases in the number of students in poverty and in the number of students qualifying for special education services. At the same time, many of these districts are also experiencing decreases in support staff, administration, and teachers as they try to do more with less.

Superintendents and school boards have been tasked with raising student test scores and demanding that school personnel be more accountable for student learning. In many states, they have been given this task in an environment of decreasing state funding and a tax-weary local public. School board members are asked to make critical decisions about finances, budgets, tax rates, and policy direction, and they rely on the superintendent to guide them in this high-stakes decision making.

Federal and state contexts affect the superintendency, especially the pressures associated with the position. Federal legislation governing education has increased demands for higher student test scores, special education services and funding, and accountability for educational professionals. States have also added additional layers to these laws and have often done so with decreased ability to provide funding and support. These federal and state contexts are a source of conflict for superintendents with boards, internal audiences, and external publics.

Although these state and national contexts are not the focus of this book, it is important to acknowledge their influence because they have an enormous impact on how schools are run and students are taught in today's educational system. Arguably, these contexts are at least a contributing factor in some way in most superintendent departures, and even though they may not be the immediate focus of the discussion at hand, they are never far from consideration or impact.

ORGANIZATION OF THE BOOK

Chapters 2, 3, and 4 contain three detailed scenarios that, based on our research and experience, represent a variety of common issues, contexts, and problems that superintendents typically face. Two of the scenarios involve superintendents in the process of considering whether it is time to make an unanticipated departure. The third scenario involves a superintendent who has already undergone the unanticipated departure process. He is reflecting on the experience from the perspective of a new superintendency and an opportunity to teach a university-level course in educational leadership. The stories do not reflect the experiences per se of any one research source or superintendent. Real-life situations are referenced but are modified to create a composite experience that reflects our research and protects the anonymity of participants.

Annotated resources support the scenarios. The superintendents used these resources to guide them as things in their districts became more difficult. One scenario focuses on current books of interest, one scenario focuses on articles, and the last scenario focuses on books commonly used as textbooks for graduate study. While this organization is a bit contrived from the perspective of how a person would research in real life, it is intended to help orient the reader to the types of materials available in each format and, it is hoped, will make the references easier for readers to use.

Chapter 5 describes the process we used in interviewing the twenty-two superintendents, as well as the demographic information related to the group. In addition, the chapter contains descriptions and interpretations of two frameworks that evolved as data from the interviews were analyzed. The first framework looks at commonalities that were found among superintendents at various stages in their leadership tenure (years of service as a superintendent). The second framework breaks down the unanticipated superintendent departure into four phases: (1) preparation, (2) recognition, (3) management, and (4) recovery and reflection.

In chapter 6, the lessons learned from the superintendents' experiences as reflected in the two frameworks presented in chapter 5 are discussed in depth. The interviews yielded a tremendous amount of practical advice that stands on its own as important information for current and aspiring superintendents regarding unanticipated departures. That is, the advice led to key findings and lessons that we believe will be helpful to readers.

However, the collective effect of the advice and information was the substance from which the patterns, commonalities of experiences, and differences in stages (in both frameworks) emerged to provide greater value than the sum of the raw information. We believe that this relatively small project, with twenty-two subjects, is a pithy but pertinent sample that should be tested with a larger sample size in the future.

We are so very grateful to the twenty-two superintendents who agreed to be part of this project. They were not paid, and they knew there would be no formal recognition for their participation in this book. Their valuable insights and experiences made this book possible. These unassuming yet dynamic leaders are the epitome of Badaracco's definition of "quiet leaders" (2002). He states that it is important that we "look away from great figures, extreme situations, and moments of high historical drama and pay closer attention to people around us" (p. 5). The twenty-two superintendents who participated in this project are truly "the people around us" who make important differences in the lives of others every day. These quiet leaders (not to be equated with quiet people!) are the leaders that others look up to and emulate, and it is the wisdom of these quiet leaders that we believe is most valuable to others who may experience an unanticipated departure.

Chapter Two

The Story of Roberta K.

Roberta sat back in the beat-up leather chair in her office as the late afternoon sun streamed in the window. As she studied a small spider on the ceiling above the drab conference table in the middle of the crowded office, she made note of how truly exhausted she felt and wondered what to do next. Her superintendency in the Southfield district had started three years ago with a high level of support, optimism, and a sense of collaboration from the board, central office staff, building principals, and community. Now, it felt like these stakeholders were on a "witch hunt" and nothing she did was right.

Often, the criticisms were public—comments made by board members, editorials, and citizen comments in the *Southfield Messenger*—but lately, Roberta had noticed changes in the climate and mood of building principals and central office staff during meetings and casual conversations. People were certainly still very polite and professional, but there was a new tension in the air. The questions asked were focused less on moving the district's long-range plan forward and more on the immediate problems at hand.

It seemed that there was often more complaining and venting than problem solving and collaboration. She had tried every strategy she could think of to try to bring back some of the old sense of teamwork and camaraderie. Some of the central office and building principals seemed to feel sorry for her. Others showed as much support as they could, while still others always seemed to be just ending very private and meaningful conversations the moment she entered a room.

When Roberta had considered applying for the superintendency in Southfield three years ago, she was a forty-eight-year-old divorcée with two children in college. The position was several hundred miles from her residence in Northfield, but she had been working hard as a central office administrator in the Northfield school district and going to school evenings and weekends to earn her doctorate and obtain her superintendent's certification. Her dissertation centered on issues related to adequacy funding (Odden & Picus, 2007), so when the position opened up in Southfield, a local search firm believed her philosophies and credentials would be a good fit for the district.

When Roberta interviewed for the position, the board was most concerned about looming budget shortfalls and increasing student achievement as measured by state tests. She had explained her philosophy of approaching school budgeting from an adequacy perspective and explained that her five-year plan for the district included possible revisions regarding the ways non-instructional services were delivered, particularly in the areas of food service and maintenance. The capstone of her plan for the district was updating and upgrading all aspects of technology to make the district more competitive in a 21st-century learning environment.

Roberta was hired and immediately began to implement her vision for improving student achievement; she ultimately saved money by having the district become more technologically savvy, moving to online textbooks, integrating Smartboards and other technology tools into classroom instruction, and making more information available to parents and community members through a plan that involved teacher and administrator input on the school's website. When Roberta was hired, the board informed her that she was chosen over other candidates for her forward-thinking budget ideas and her emphasis on technology as a means of improving student achievement.

For the first eighteen months of her tenure as superintendent, things seemed to go well. She met with the board, administrative team, and teacher-leaders to develop a long-range plan that incorporated many of the cost-saving measures associated with adequacy funding and focused on improving student achievement through increased use of technology.

The local media was very excited about these plans and gave the district positive coverage and ample opportunities to speak on local talk radio shows. Civic groups asked her to come to explain her new vision for the district, and these plans were well received. Before she became superintendent, the previous superintendent had encouraged central office staff to apply for technology grants, and one of the grants applied for was awarded to the district during the early months of her tenure, providing all of the elementary schools in the district with Smartboards, although training was not included in the grant. As Roberta reflected back on these first eighteen months as superintendent, she now realized that it was truly a "honeymoon" phase.

In the late fall of her second year as superintendent, the first hints of the problems she was to face in the coming months began to surface. The budget shortfall in the first year was in line with the projections, but there was already strong evidence that this year's budget shortfall would be significantly larger than anyone had anticipated. Although several small steps had been taken to reduce costs in the district (including a reduction in instructional aides, purchasing energy futures, and retrofitting all building with energy-efficient lighting), her vision for outsourcing food service and maintenance services was stalling. Two of the board members had a mutual close friend who was a long-time custodian in the district, and even though it was explained to these board members that their friend would very likely still have a position in the district, they balked at the change in the structure of the services, especially regarding the changes in insurance and benefits that would result from using an outsourcing approach to providing these services.

Many problems were surfacing regarding the incorporation of online textbooks, most notably with computer access in the schools. Roberta understood that an initial investment in computer equipment in the classrooms would be necessary to realize the savings in using online materials, but the board was reluctant to approve the expenditures.

Several principals were beginning to express frustration that Smartboards were underutilized or unused altogether in classrooms because staff were not adequately trained in how to incorporate them effectively into lesson plans, and professional development budgets and contract time for principal-directed professional development requirements were already stretched too thin.

Roberta had anticipated many of these problems and was working through them in her second year, confident that solutions could be found that aligned with the new long-range goals of reducing costs and improving student achievement. In the spring of her second year, two new board members were elected, and two of her best supporters for outsourcing services were no longer on the board. One had decided not to run for reelection for personal reasons, and the other lost in the election, yet another telling indication that public support for her initiatives was perhaps starting to wane.

In the fall of Roberta's third year as superintendent, a policy issue arose that placed the school district in the center of media attention and deeply divided the community. For several years, the district had maintained a "no cell phone" policy for students while at school. This policy was creating an undue amount of work for assistant principals and school office staff, as the process of confiscating cell phones, calling parents, and arranging for them to pick up cell phones was taking an inordinate amount of time.

Many principals and assistant principals expressed concern that cell phone management was taking away from other important disciplinary issues, while others expressed strong beliefs that the policy should remain in place. Roberta was aware that opinions on this issue were changing nationally, with an often-expressed belief that cell phones and other student technology could be used to enhance instruction. She supported a change in the cell phone policy that would allow students to use their cell phones before and after school and during the lunch hour. Cell phones were to be off during the school day unless a teacher had expressly written the use of cell phones into the lesson plan.

When this policy change was first presented to the board, it created almost immediate upheaval in the district. Board members and the community were as divided as administrators on the issue. A local talk radio host devoted several segments to discussion of the policy, taking many calls from local citizens. Roberta was beginning to realize that her public support was far from universal. One citizen called her the "technology superintendent" that was going to "run the district into the ground with all of her technology spending."

Parents flooded the website with comments ranging from threats to pull students out of the district if the new policy passed to threats to pull students out of the district if it did not pass. Roberta was surprised and shaken by the intensity and interest in this policy change, but she knew this challenge was to be expected and she felt that she could handle it with her experience and training. She went to the newspaper and local talk radio shows and explained the advantages of the new policy.

The vote on the policy was scheduled for the following board meeting. Roberta moved the venue of the board meeting to a larger meeting space to accommodate the anticipated increase in audience turnout due to the high interest in the issue. The meeting was moved to the high school auditorium, which was filled to capacity at meeting time. After many citizen comments and a great deal of debate, the nine-member board passed the new cell phone policy with a 5–4 vote. Two of the members who had voted against the cell phone policy were the new board members. Roberta felt she had won an important victory and went home that evening feeling on top of the world.

Roberta's enjoyment of this victory was short-lived. Soon, the collateral effects of the fight to pass the cell phone policy became evident as the district continued to pursue its long-range goals. Roberta was quickly cementing a reputation as a superintendent who was willing to spend resources on technology but little else. Resistance to outsourcing increased dramatically from the two new board members, who were bitter about the change in the cell phone policy. When the proposed budget was presented to the board in the late winter, any new technology expenditures were immediately voted down.

Board members were instructing her to find alternative ways of cutting costs, including reducing building budgets, supply budgets, and increasing class sizes. They questioned the reduction in aides, believing that adding aides would allow for increased class sizes. What Roberta only later realized was that the board was making the same suggestions for budget cuts that they made under the previous superintendent. While some cost savings could be realized through these types of measures, Roberta also knew that they would not result in enough savings to offset the anticipated budget reductions.

Roberta's problems in the winter of her third year were not limited to the board. The teachers' union was resisting many of Roberta's initiatives. District-wide training for Smartboards and other new technology investments had still not occurred because there was not contract time available to mandate it. Roberta had made three separate attempts to require teachers to post lesson plans and student progress reports online for parents to view, but teachers refused, saying it was an additional duty and must be compensated either with extra pay or reduction of other duties. As a result, only a handful of teachers provided information to parents on the district website that fulfilled the goals of the district's long-range plan.

The media was increasingly questioning whether the district was behaving in a fiscally responsible manner and moving in the right direction. There were increased requests from the media for documentation related to test scores. Roberta's requests to appear on a local talk radio show to discuss new initiatives was sometimes denied or postponed. Invitations from civic groups stopped coming, and significantly more comments were being left on the district website questioning every decision Roberta made.

Roberta's problems were capped off by declines in student achievement. Two schools in the district did not make Adequate Yearly Progress (AYP) for the first time in the district's history. While one other school had not made AYP the year before she arrived, this school had made good improvements in her first year and students were showing enough academic improvement to make AYP the following year. This fact did nothing to deter outcry from the public and the board about the two other schools.

In this, the spring of her third year, Roberta's confidence had waned and she felt like she was engaged in damage control full time. She had reached out to her mentor from graduate school and other superintendents in the area. She had talked to a few close friends and even her children about the situation, and while they listened patiently and sympathized, they could offer little advice. Finally, at the regional meeting of superintendents, she explained many of her difficulties to her colleagues, and many of them approached her afterwards with words of encouragement and advice. Nothing seemed to help.

One of Roberta's colleagues had given her a few books, which sat on the kitchen counter of her nicely appointed condo. As she sat thinking in her office, Roberta realized that the spider had long since moved to begin constructing a web in a more advantageous spot and the standard-issue round white clock with its large black numbers read 6:30. Roberta decided it was time to go home. In her first year at Southfield, she would have stayed at least another hour, double-checking her e-mail, reviewing her calendar for the next day, and making notes on how the day went and what she wanted to accomplish tomorrow. Now, when the day was over, Roberta was more than ready to go home.

Normally, on a night like tonight, Roberta would stop for takeout at her favorite sandwich shop or Chinese restaurant, but tonight she didn't feel like running into anyone who might want to stop to talk to her about some district-related issue. Roberta headed home, where her gray-and-white tabby, Simon, greeted her at the door with a meow that meant he was out of food. She fed Simon and went to change into her comfortable and comforting lounge clothes. In her bedroom, she noticed the two growing piles of laundry that were accumulating in the corner, one for the dry cleaner and one to do at home. She looked in the mirror and noticed that it was time to make an appointment at the salon to get her hair done.

Roberta knew that a professional appearance was important in her position, yet it seemed more and more difficult to keep it up with all of the stress. She went into the living room and turned on the television to the Food Network, then went into the kitchen to fix a frozen dinner. Roberta loved to cook, but it was a luxury that she didn't have the time or energy for anymore. As the frozen dinner cooked in the microwave, Roberta considered the books on the counter that her colleague had given her at the superintendents' regional meeting. "My kitchen counter is for book storage, not food prep," she thought to herself wryly.

The titles were ominous: *The Anguish of Leadership* (Patterson, 2000), *The Wounded Leader* (Ackerman, 2002), *Resilient Leaders* (Patterson & Kelleher, 2005), and *The Dark Side of Educational Leadership* (Polka & Litchka, 2008). When Roberta first received these books, she was grateful, but had a sense of dread at the message her colleague was sending her. Now, as she stood in front of the microwave feeling wounded, resistant, and hopeless, Roberta knew it was time to take in what these books had to say.

Roberta took her dinner out of the microwave and fixed herself a gin and tonic. She took the books and food into the living room, turned down the volume on the television, and sat down to eat and read. After two hours, the dinner had long since been eaten, another drink poured, and Roberta was absorbed in the books.

The first book that Roberta read was *The Anguish of Leadership* (Patterson, 2000). Patterson's work on superintendent departures has been extensive. He consistently emphasizes the need for superintendents to learn from a departure and move forward, ultimately resulting in an individual who will have greater strength, experience, and optimism in his or her next superintendency. Roberta read the compelling stories of the highs and lows of fourteen high-profile superintendents, and she was beginning to understand the message that her colleague was sending in giving her these books. Was it time to find another position? Roberta had not entertained this question before. She initially felt sick about the prospect of leaving Southfield and starting over somewhere else, although a strange sense of relief was also spreading through her. She had a choice.

Roberta was quickly beginning to understand that her situation was far more commonplace than she had originally thought. Ackerman and Maslin-Ostrowski (2002) described the trials and tribulations of several superintendents in *The Wounded Leader*. She read and related to the stories of difficult political situations and of superintendents trying to work with and for boards that were becoming increasingly more difficult. While none of the case studies mirrored her situation exactly, Roberta related to each of the superintendent stories in different ways. Her frustration and pain was beginning to wane as it was being replaced by a desire to seek different kinds of answers than she had previously sought.

Next, Roberta read *The Dark Side of Educational Leadership* (Polka & Litchka, 2008). Although she found the title particularly intimidating, she read a description of "professional victim syndrome" that occurs during times of crisis and realized that it was a mind-set that she was wearing more and more often in recent weeks. Had her situation at the district risen to the level of crisis? She began to believe so. As she continued to read, she began to understand how important it was not to marginalize her own feelings and to continue to reach out and seek support as she had done at her last regional superintendent's meeting.

Patterson and Kelleher's (2005) *Resilient School Leaders* was particularly helpful in framing her situation in a positive manner as she read about the four phases of the resilience cycle: (1) deteriorating, (2) adapting, (3) recovering, and (4) growing. Using this framework, Roberta was able to see how there might be light at the end of the dark tunnel in which she currently found herself. She saw herself currently in the deterioration stage and perhaps ready to move into the adapting phase. As she read on, Roberta also began to understand that the things she was experiencing now would make her a better leader in the future—probably somewhere else.

Over the next several days, Roberta continued to read the books that her colleague had given her. She began to look at her problems from a different frame of reference. Roberta realized how much she was concerned about her own career and future, and not only about solving the problems of the district. As she wondered what to do next, the possibilities had expanded in recent days to include moving herself out of this position for which she had fought so hard. She contemplated trying to establish a vision and achieve her goals in a different district.

Most importantly, she took a step back to reflect in a brutal and honest way about the current situation in the district. She asked herself several difficult questions, and she realized that the answers she had for those questions were very different now than they would have been six months earlier.

STUDY/DISCUSSION QUESTIONS

1. What did Roberta do well during her first two years as superintendent at Southfield School District?
2. What might Roberta have done differently during her first two years as superintendent at Southfield School District?
3. Do you think Roberta represents a "typical" new superintendent? If so, in what ways? That is, what was Roberta experiencing in her personal and professional life that you as a superintendent might expect to experience?
4. Do you agree with the way Roberta handled the technology issues in the district? Do you think that she rightfully earned her reputation as the "technology superintendent"? What would you do the same or differently?
5. Did Roberta manage the cell phone policy issue correctly? Was the passage of the cell phone policy worth the "political capital" that it cost? If yes, why? If no, is there any issue that might be worth using such political capital?
6. After reading chapters 5 and 6, does Roberta's situation fit the Superintendent Experience Framework? If so, how? If not, why not?
7. After reading chapters 5 and 6, how many stages of the Unanticipated Departure Framework can you identify in Roberta's scenario? Which stage is Roberta experiencing at the end of the scenario? What advice would you have for Roberta based on the key findings of the framework?

ROBERTA'S BOOK REVIEW

Dr. Jerry Patterson, *The Anguish of Leadership* (2000)

Patterson's portrayal of the superintendency describes the "good, bad, and ugly" of superintendent leadership and includes several case studies examining rocky departures. Specifically, Patterson initiated a request to the American Association of School Administrators (AASA) for the opportunity to write a book about the positives and negatives of the superintendency. AASA suggested fourteen superintendents, each of whom was near the end of a very successful, high-profile career. Patterson believed these superintendents had unique wisdom as a result of their experience (250 years collectively) and their impressive accomplishments in twenty-eight superintendencies, primarily serving urban districts. In addition, these superintendents had at least some degree of diversity, and included eight males, six females, two African American superintendents, and one Hispanic superintendent.

Each of the fourteen superintendents is described as having led "complex and diverse education systems and is among the acknowledged leaders in the profession" (p. x). In addition to being held in high regard, these superintendents enjoyed a relatively smooth and stable superintendency for a sustained period of time, some for two years and others up to twenty-five years. After this period of relative calm, most of the fourteen superintendents encountered a period of significant turmoil.

The stories of these fourteen superintendents are most compelling. The triumphs and tribulations of each individual provide a tremendous living history and unique insight into the role that superintendents fill. Their stories are a tribute to the daily and yearly struggles superintendents face as they undertake their roles and responsibilities in school districts across the nation. Patterson writes that most of the fourteen superintendents experienced "the erosion of the board support, [which] lead to frustrations great and small that piled up along the way" (p. 21).

Patterson makes an important point by addressing the effects of "rocks in your pockets." The idea behind this familiar leadership metaphor is that small rocks (problems) collected in a pocket over time add up to an overwhelming burden that eventually weighs down and immobilizes an individual. The accumulation of small problems inhibits a superintendent by degrees as years in a district accumulate. Eventually, the effect of too many "rocks in your pockets" may result in the need for a change in superintendents.

The superintendents featured in this book did not start in a climate of "rocks" or difficulty. Patterson indicates that each of the superintendents was hired to address "major, complex problems in their new district" (p. 23). He writes that the superintendents experienced many good times, which were characterized by three conditions: (1) a supportive board president, (2) a strong board nucleus, and (3) stable board composition.

Patterson writes that in most cases difficulty occurred when the board support started to erode. This erosion was highlighted with the aforementioned "rocks in pockets" analogy. Patterson states that several of the superintendents talked openly and emotionally about the defining last issues that became their downfall (p. 37). He describes this final stage as "when the last rock is a boulder" (p. 36).

Patterson transforms the bad experiences into the ugly side of the superintendency, describing this phenomenon as the "human toll of leadership" (p. 47). He provides anecdotal reports from many of the fourteen superintendents about the heavy personal and family toll involved during times of turmoil. Many superintendents reported significant declines in their physical health and mental well-being, which they would often try to deny or marginalize. However, several superintendents indicated that watching the family suffer as a result of the turmoil was the most difficult part of the experience.

Advice is also provided for superintendents, titled "Words from the Wise" (p. 53). The chapter is divided into two major sections dealing with preparation for being a superintendent and how to best serve as a superintendent. Advice on preparation for the superintendency includes: (1) seeking broad-based experience, (2) finding a good mentor (or two), (3) getting off to a good start, (4) knowing that you cannot know it all, and (5) providing special advice for women and minority leaders.

Good advice is also provided for acting superintendents and includes: (1) build positive board/superintendent relationships; (2) negotiate board/superintendent roles; (3) maintain trust and confidentiality; (4) promote positive community relations; (5) work with, not against, the union; and (6) befriend the media.

Finally, Patterson provides a brief but critical section in the final chapter entitled "When Moving On" (p. 66). He sets the stages for this topic by stating the following:

> People leave jobs all the time. But exiting very few jobs involves the same visibility and political fall-out as leaving the superintendency. Most superintendents I interviewed have left at least one superintendency. Whether their exit was voluntary or not, and whether they were moving on to another superintendency, making a career change, or retiring, their reflections make clear that exiting can be a difficult process. (p. 66)

Three ideas superintendents should consider as part of the exit strategy include:

- Knowing when to "fold 'em"
- Looking for another superintendency
- Seeking closure

In addition to the timeless, valuable advice, Patterson writes eleven "best of" wisdom bits for readers (p. 70). He concludes his book by stating the importance of serving students and for superintendents to hold onto the core values that initially compelled them to the superintendency.

Richard H. Ackerman and Pat Maslin-Ostrowski, *The Wounded Leader: How Real Leadership Emerges in Times of Crisis* (2002)

Ackerman and Maslin-Ostrowski use a "case story" approach to focus on the difficult circumstances individual educational leaders have faced and how they addressed a significant crisis in their experience. According to Ackerman and Maslin-Ostrowski:

> A case story is a description, both written and oral, or a real-life, close-to-the-bone leadership situation, written with words meant to come fully to life when discussed. In contrast to the familiar case study, in which the participant learns vicariously through other people's cases, the case story approach invites people to learn through writing and telling their own personal experience as practitioners. (p. xx)

The authors contacted sixty-five administrators who encountered difficulty and reported on four educational leaders (two principals, two superintendents) in their book. The sample was based on a personal network of contacts.

The two superintendent case stories highlighted in *The Wounded Leader* focus on the relevant and familiar "push and pull" situations in which superintendents often find themselves. One of the case stories deals with the required response an urban superintendent must give in addressing a desegregation case against the wishes of a school board. The second case story outlines a common situation in which a veteran superintendent must deal with new board members, which results in a "new" board. The struggle of the superintendent to maintain direction in the district clashes with the board's desire to move in a different direction.

Superintendent One had been successful in two districts prior to the position in which he encountered difficulty. As a result of his description of board resistance, he described two major trials. The first trial was that of family stress and turmoil. The second trial was the cynicism that resulted from the crush of extraordinarily difficult politics. The superintendent described this as the "darker side of school politics" (p. 45).

Superintendent Two started to experience difficulty in the district in which he was promoted in his fourth year. He described the changes in the board as including a new board chair and several new board members. The superintendent describes the internal conflict of trying "to satisfy" the board but continuously having conflict (p. 86). This led to feeling wary and unsupported. Eventually, the superintendent returned to a position as a principal where he found great satisfaction.

Ackerman and Maslin-Ostrowski provide much direction for aspiring and current superintendents in dealing with the wounds that one can suffer in a leadership position. One of the major lessons is to learn from the experience and reach the point of being a better person for the experience. The authors label this lesson as "leadership growth" (p. 103).

There are other clear lessons to be learned if you are a wounded educational leader as described by Ackerman and Maslin-Ostrowski. For example, the authors write that there is no way to prepare for the experience (p. 4). They describe the effects that can result when an educational leader begins to doubt his or her own leadership ability. This lack of trust in "their own leadership" is considered the "beginning of the wound" (p. 4). As a result of the wounding process starting, there is typically a "significant collision with the organizational environment" that leads to "conflict, anguish, and more" (p. 5). This turmoil leads to vulnerability, especially in the superintendency (p. 27). The authors describe this as a riptide and state that no school leader should be considered immune from its power.

As with each of the four books cited in this section, Ackerman and Maslin-Ostrowski conclude on a hopeful note and provide advice for education leaders. Almost forty pages are devoted to general and specific suggestions for dealing with the healing process. A clear and brief statement of healing lessons is listed here:

- Learn to trust the unattended areas of your leadership—especially your feelings.
- Listen honestly and deeply for the questions that are feared or left out of your work life altogether.
- Find folks to talk to whom you really trust (p. 107).

Walter S. Polka and Peter R. Litchka, *The Dark Side of Educational Leadership* (2008)

As former superintendents and current college professors teaching educational administration, the authors surveyed almost 500 superintendents in Georgia and the state of New York. As a result of the survey, fifty superintendents were described as experiencing "professional victim syndrome" (PVS). Of the fifty professional victims, thirty were selected for follow-up interviews in the research study on which the book is based. The sample consisted of ten females and twenty males. Seventeen served in small districts (1,000 students or less), five served in medium districts (1,000–5,000), and eight served in large districts. Twenty-five of the thirty professional victims were first- or second-time superintendents.

Polka and Litchka used Ackerman and Maslin-Ostrowski's definition of professional victim syndrome in their research (2002). Professional victim syndrome occurs as the result of a crisis event in the superintendency that is "wound[ing] . . . to the core, attacking . . . identity or integrity—the very soul of a person's way of being" (p. 193). This crisis event is typically the result of a buildup of conditions conducive to crisis and includes board members micromanaging, a disagreement and disappointment by a board over a personal decision, budget issues, or misuse of power by board members. Usually, a combination of issues eventually led to an erupting crisis.

Polka and Litchka articulate their pertinent findings in one particularly informative section of the book. Some of the more significant and compelling findings include:

- A one-vote margin is important, and ultimately the board, not the superintendent, owns the district (p. viii).
- Most of the PVS superintendents became stronger personally and professionally after working through PVS.
- In hindsight, some of the PVS superintendents believed they were too stubborn in the time of crisis.
- The authors outline guidance on how to deal with the crisis. They have a belief that current and future PVS superintendents have (or will have) the knowledge, skills, and dispositions necessary to lead our schools during times of personal and professional crisis (pp. 159–62).

Finally Polka and Litchka provide additional guidance for superintendents and include several suggestions: (1) constantly reflect on professional/personal choices/actions, (2) maintain close personal relationships and friendships, and (3) maintain self-care in a caring environment (pp. 167–68).

Jerry Patterson and Paul Kelleher, *Resilient School Leaders* (2005)

This book focuses on the potential for a positive future when personal energy is invested wisely and one acts on the courage of conviction. It is organized using a strengths-based model. The authors encourage leaders to tap into three sources of "resilience capacity"—personal values, personal efficacy, and personal energy.

Twenty-five educational leaders and professional writers were selected for involvement in the project and collectively have "more than 700 years of . . . experience." The resources of AASA were used to solicit nominations. Fourteen of the twenty-five individuals chosen for the project had superintendent experience, primarily in urban or suburban districts. The other eleven participants in the study are well-known researchers and writers in education.

Patterson and Kelleher provide a comprehensive description of the theoretical model when describing in detail the model of resilience they apply to understanding educational leaders. Briefly, they define resilience as "using your energy productively to emerge from adversity stronger than ever." There are three dimensions to resilience: current and future interpretation of adversity, capacity to address adversity, and the actions required to address adversity.

The authors describe four phases of the resilience cycle that educational leaders move through when they encounter adversity (p. 12). The phases begin after "a disruption" to what Patterson and Kelleher call "normal conditions" (p. 13). The four phases include: (1) deteriorating, (2) adapting, (3) recovering, and (4) growing. A short summary of the emotions that characterize each phase follows:

- Deteriorating: characterized by anger, aggression, feeling like a victim, becoming your own worst enemy, blame, degradation, denial, grief
- Adapting: characterized by less anger and denial than deteriorating; assuming a victim role; do not plateau in "survival mode"
- Recovering: characterized by emotional maintenance; returning to emotional state before adversity occurred
- Growing: characterized by thriving in "a sustained level of strengthened resilience" and a "rational optimism" in their circumstances (p. 15)

Optimism is a core concept of resilience. Patterson and Kelleher make a strong connection between optimism and success. Optimistic individuals are described as having a number of common attributes, including positive social relationships, generally better health, the ability to recover from setbacks, viewing adversity as a challenge, working hard, and having high morals, perseverance, and a high level of motivation.

A final feature of this book is the recounting of details regarding how the twenty-five leaders addressed adversity in their personal lives and as professional educators. The authors identify and describe six strengths of resilient leaders and connect the narratives of the twenty-five resilient leaders to the six strengths. These six strengths are:

1. Accurately assess past and current reality
2. Are positive about future possibilities
3. Remain true to personal values
4. Maintain a strong sense of personal efficacy
5. Invest personal energy wisely
6. Act on the courage of personal convictions

This book is an important contribution to the literature on leadership challenges and overcoming adversity in a leadership role. Focusing on optimism and cultivating strengths enabled the twenty-five participants and the authors to share the positive attributes of their leadership experiences, although it is in the context of working through difficulty.

Chapter Three

The Story of Richard B.

The 5:30 a.m. alarm rang. Richard reached over to turn it off, fully awake as he had been nearly every morning for the past thirty-two years. He went through his ritualistic morning routine, inflexible in its execution except when a district emergency arose. After showering and shaving, he went into the closet and took the next suit in rotation off the rack, pairing it with a starched white shirt still in the bag from the dry cleaner.

His wife, Sarah, slept soundly through this routine. In previous years, she would have dozed lightly while he readied for the day ahead and gotten up shortly before he left the house to get herself ready for the day. Now that she was retired, she found that she enjoyed sleeping in the morning and frequently did not get up until after he left the house.

Richard watched Sarah sleep, and he was glad that she was able to enjoy this indulgence in retirement. For many years, she had worked tirelessly in her job as an accountant, then as assistant vice president for a large manufacturing firm. His mind quickly turned from this comforting thought to the day ahead and the burning issues in the district. He worked hard to compartmentalize these thoughts so that district problems did not consume him. It was important that he was able to enjoy at least a little bit of every day with Sarah and his family. Richard firmly believed that this approach to the superintendency was one of the reasons that he had generally been successful in the position over the past eleven years.

As Richard left the house, he noted in passing that once again he felt a tug of desire for retirement, when he and Sarah could actually do many of the things that they now talked and dreamed about. Richard had turned fifty-nine in September and wanted to work another two years in order to take full advantage of his retirement options through the district.

Richard's plan seemed like a sound one; however, there were concerns about Sarah's health since she had been recently diagnosed with diabetes. Although she seemed fine most of the time, she was under her doctor's close supervision. Richard did not want to think about the future without her, and whether Sarah was sick or not, the trips to the doctor and constant monitoring were glaring reminders that their time together was finite.

When Richard neared the district offices, his thoughts rapidly changed to the pressing issues that were weighing heavily on his mind. As he drove, he took a small series of detours that had become his new habit. For the past eleven years, Richard arrived at work promptly at 7:10 a.m. each morning. Since the last elections, the new board president had used the occasion of his early morning arrival to come in unannounced and criticize his stance on any number of issues. She often demanded changes in the board agenda and requested increasing amounts of paperwork, most of which required significant staff hours to generate and were seldom actually used in any board decision-making processes.

Richard's secretary, Judy, was at her desk by 7:30 a.m. Richard used to relish the twenty minutes or so before her arrival, using the time to organize his thoughts and his day, and tending to little tasks that would not get attention at any other time during the day. Now, he only felt anxious and vulnerable during this time, so he arrived at 7:25 a.m., just in time to get to his office before Judy arrived.

His precious twenty minutes were now mostly spent taking random detours and stopping for a cup of coffee at a local convenience store. Richard felt that he still had to leave the house at the same time as he always did, so that his wife would not worry that something was wrong. These problems were his problems, and these board members were his board members. He had handled them before, and he would handle them now.

There was something different about the atmosphere in central office, though, and it was hard for Richard to identify it. The obvious answer was the turnover on the board. The current board was the first that had none of the members who had hired him eleven years ago. Now, the longest serving board members had been on the board for five years. Recently, two new board members had replaced two who had decided to retire from board service.

The board members who had retired were instrumental in supporting many of the initiatives and improvements that the district had implemented in the past decade. Busy professionals with school-age children replaced these experienced board members. They had limited time for attending workshops, in-services, and other professional development opportunities. Indeed, these two new board members seemed to rely largely on their professional expertise, since it seemed evident during board meetings that they spent little time reading the board packet and familiarizing themselves with the issues.

Richard missed his two departed veteran board members. Although they were full of questions and disagreements, they seemed to have had the best interests of the district and the students at heart. They were reasonable, smart people with good intentions. The two new board members and the board president were a different story altogether. The two new members were acquaintances of the board president, and she had encouraged them to run.

The board president, in her fourth year on the board, had an agenda of cutting costs and lowering taxes, yet believed that the district should not have to sacrifice anything because of these cuts. One of the new board members was adamant about cutting costs in the areas of administration and athletics. In her quest to reveal district excesses, the board president demanded a zero-based budgeting process and required ridiculous justification to the board for requests of even the smallest expenditures.

Richard thought he was managing the board president and the new board members effectively, using every possible opportunity to educate them on nonnegotiable, fixed expenses, and carefully reviewing any new requests or renewals of optional expenses. He stressed the educational importance of new and existing programs, highlighting the benefits for students, particularly disadvantaged students in the district.

Richard talked a great deal about the district's history of educational excellence and community support, and did his best to encourage the board to uphold this tradition. He also was doing his best to implement the five-year strategic plan that had been developed over two years earlier. Richard honored the board's requests for expenditure justification, and the district had begun what promised to be a long and arduous process of zero-based budgeting that was anticipated to take two years.

Despite Richard's best efforts, approval requests for any new or renewing initiatives were summarily denied, unless it could be shown that they could be implemented with virtually no cost to the district. When the board approved a tax levy significantly below the maximum allowable tax limit, the media and the public lauded the board for their fiscally responsible and conservative approach to taxation. However, all of these actions spelled problems for Richard, especially when an unanticipated problem arose with the district's technology infrastructure.

About six months ago, all of the district's computers went down. Most of the computer access, including teacher access to teaching materials and student grades, were down for two weeks. Due to the emergency nature of the problem, Richard authorized a team of consultants to come in to assess and fix the problems. The consultants determined that the entire technology infrastructure was badly outdated and heavily overloaded.

The problems were worse than Richard had anticipated. None of the schools had adequate computer capacity to serve more than one classroom at a time, and with increasing class sizes, it was becoming difficult to accommodate even one class. Richard knew that a referendum to update technology would be a hard sell for this board and the public, but without it, the district could not offer students, staff, parents, and the community the basics of a 21st-century education that they had come to expect.

In the weeks that followed the computer crisis, the board demanded a proposal from the superintendent within one month's time that would address the problem. After one month, Richard reported to the board that he needed more time. The board granted the extension but not without several rude comments from the new board members and the board president.

As Richard reflected back on this meeting, he realized that this was the first real indication that this board might have problems and issues that he might not be able to solve. He also began to feel that the board had a real sense of resentment bordering on disdain toward him that exhibited personal undertones. In short, Richard was beginning to feel like he was being set up to fail. This sensation was one he had not felt before in his eleven years as superintendent.

In his district of 5,400 students, Richard's research indicated that a $15-million referendum to be repaid over five years would enable the district to completely rebuild the entire technology infrastructure. This plan ensured adequate capacity for at least ten years in addition to equipping all of the schools' computer labs to accommodate up to two classes at a time.

Richard carefully crafted a proposal to the board and presented it during a board meeting ten weeks after the board's initial request for a proposal. The issue had cooled somewhat with the public now that computers were functional in buildings; however, there was still a fair amount of public interest in the condition of the technology infrastructure in the district, especially from key business stakeholders.

The board listened intently to the proposal. The first question from one of the new board members was how much had the district spent in hiring outside consultants to temporarily fix the computer problem and assess the condition of the overall system. Another asked how long the temporary fixes could be expected to last. Although it was a challenging evening, Richard succeeded in maintaining a sense of urgency regarding the rebuild, and the board agreed to vote the referendum up or down within the next two months.

During the time between the proposal of the referendum and the board vote, a few strange things began to happen with the board, particularly with the board president. The board president began questioning every aspect of the referendum, forcing Richard to defend the district's position in every conversation. The referendum was becoming something that the superintendent wanted, not the board, and the superintendent was expected to expend political capital to get it.

The board president began using the referendum as a political chess piece to negotiate budget cuts in other areas, particularly in athletics and administration. The conversations shifted over several weeks from question-and-answer sessions between Richard and the board president to bargaining sessions. The shift was subtle, and no threats or promises were ever overtly made; however, the message was clear. If Richard wanted continued board support for the referendum, he was going to have to recommend cuts in athletics and administration, and he was going to have to take the heat from the public for recommending those cuts.

When the board convened to vote on the referendum eight weeks later, there was much public debate on exactly how much the board should authorize for the referendum. In the end, the board approved the referendum for $12 million to be repaid over five years. This amount would cover the new technology infrastructure and allow for some limited hardware capacity increase in the school buildings. It was not as much as Richard had hoped for, but it was enough and would hopefully be an easier sell to the voting public than the $15-million option.

The month since that vote had been anything but easy for Richard. The two new board members and board president, who had voted to approve the referendum, seemed to be trying to defeat it every chance they got. It was going to be a long stretch to the spring elections. Richard knew that somehow the technology infrastructure in the district desperately needed upgrading, and he was not sure how he would be able to achieve this goal without the referendum. He wondered if the next best option was to make sure that a technology component was included in the next district strategic plan to formalize the urgency.

In addition to referendums and budgets, some board members were unhappy with the district's high school principal. There was regular pressure to nonrenew this principal, even though her performance reviews had been excellent. She had a tough, no-nonsense demeanor that was one of the key reasons Richard had hired her for the position. He felt that what she brought to the table was exactly what the school needed. And, according to the data, Richard was right. The school had seen dramatic improvements in student achievement, attendance, referrals, and law enforcement involvement since she had started as principal four years ago.

However, she managed to upset a large group of influential parents at the school when she did not give them or their children preferential treatment for parent/teacher conferences and when she made extra efforts to get low-income students involved in the school's fine arts programs. Her efforts were extremely successful. More low-income parents than ever before attended parent/teacher conferences, and the fine arts programs at the school were filled to capacity and beyond because so many more students were involved.

The success of her inclusion initiative also meant that there were more students available for the limited solos, lead parts, and competition entries that were part of the fine arts program. The children of influential parents did not automatically receive these coveted positions as they had in the past. When they contacted the principal, she addressed them with the same matter-of-fact, no-nonsense tone that she used with everyone else. The situation was coming to a head because one of the new board members was also one of these influential parents, and she had run in large part to remove this principal from the school.

Richard arrived just a moment before Judy, his assistant, arrived. Both were settled in after a few minutes when the board president walked in. With a cursory hello to Judy, she walked into Richard's office unannounced. Richard had expected the board president and greeted her with the same polite coolness that he always did. However, this morning's conversation was not the normal conversation they usually had. A new subject was on the table, and it took Richard off guard.

"Have you thought that it might be time for you to retire or leave the district?" the board president asked.

"Are you unhappy with my performance?" Richard countered.

"Well, a few board members have talked to me, and I've been thinking about it, and we think it might be time for new leadership," she said flatly.

At this moment, Richard knew his days in the district were numbered. He politely asked her to give him some time to think about it and left the office, saying he had to go to another meeting. What he really had to do was get out and walk, clear his head, and get his bearings. As he walked and thought, the gravity of what was said hit him fully, and he knew he had to think and act quickly, which was not a natural thing for him to do.

One of the hardest things for Richard to process was that he was not surprised by this request. With the way his relationship with the board had deteriorated over the past year, he wondered if and when they might ask him to leave. He realized that one of the reasons he had been avoiding the board president's morning visits whenever possible was to avoid hearing what he had heard this morning. He was not sure if he was ready for such a big change, and certainly did not like the feeling of being out of control of his own future.

His thoughts quickly moved from his own future to his wife. Now, he would have to tell her how bad things had really been. He did not want to burden her with that information, and he did not want her to know that he had not confided in her because he wanted to spare her the pain and worry. He also worried about Judy and his hard-working high school principal, both of whom would likely be unemployed when he left the district. His thoughts turned to all of the wonderful people he had worked with in the last eleven years and how they had achieved so many things of which they could be proud. He wondered what direction the district would go in once he left.

Richard went back to the office and checked his calendar. He had a full schedule and spent the day buried in his work to take the morning's conversation off of his mind. Late in the afternoon, the board president sent a request to Richard and the board clerk for a closed session board meeting to discuss the future of the superintendent. Things were moving much faster than he had anticipated.

The end of day was difficult for Richard. Earlier in the morning, all he had wanted to do after his initial conversation with the board president was to go home and never come back. Now he dreaded going home, mostly because he was going to have to rehash everything he had thought and felt all day all over again as he explained the entire situation to Sarah. He took comfort in the fact that she would be supportive, but he took no comfort in his own feelings of failure and the thought that he would not be able to keep those feelings a secret from her.

Richard looked out the window at the late afternoon sun, and his eye ran over an article in the most recent issue of *The School Administrator.* He picked it up, thumbed through it, and as he did, he began to feel a surge of energy. He went to his bookshelves and grabbed a stack of journals that he had collected over the course of his career, and began to thumb through them. As he marked articles in a very purposeful manner, he began to clearly realize that he was not alone, and that his experiences were not new.

Although most of the articles were written within the past ten years, Richard pulled from the pile an article written by McCarthy and Bennet (1991) titled *If You're Fired, Here's How to Land on Your Feet.* As Richard read the article, the words in it took on a new meaning as he pondered his current situation. McCarthy writes:

> The rage I felt still smolders—18 months after I last worked as a superintendent, nine months since my last paycheck. I was forced to resign/was terminated at the beginning of my second year of a three-year contract. The official reason: philosophical differences and leadership style. (p. 14)

McCarthy describes the negative effects his resignation/termination had on future job searches and the different ways that employers in small, medium, and large districts reacted to his termination/resignation. As a large-district superintendent, small and midsize districts told him that he was overqualified and might not be provided enough challenge. Large districts viewed him as having failed already in a large school district setting. Therefore, he seemed stuck in a "no-man's land."

McCarthy also addresses the emotional and practical aspects of an unexpected resignation/termination. Officially, McCarthy was told "the board has lost confidence in your ability to serve as superintendent. You have 48 hours to vacate your office and turn in your keys" (p. 15). From a personal perspective, McCarthy reminds readers that even under these extreme conditions, it is important not to act in haste, to seek help from a good counselor, and to take time to work through the issues with your family. From a professional perspective, McCarthy describes his journey toward departure, including making contact with a trusted superintendent colleague and arranging for his own legal representation. When McCarthy had completed these steps, he arranged to meet with the board to discuss/agree to departure arrangements.

Richard found himself reassured by this advice, and as he read, he was thinking of ways to adapt this advice to fit his own situation. He was thinking that perhaps it might be time for his own departure. Recent thoughts about retirement focused on his new life after the superintendency. Now, he began to visualize all of the parts and pieces of the actual departure process. The short articles he was reading about superintendent departure gave Richard ideas about what to visualize and helped him to understand what he might expect.

As Richard read through other articles, he was reassured about what he already understood from experience: The board/superintendent match is critical to a superintendent's success (Kinsella, 2004; McAdams, 1997; Namit, 2008; Stover, 2011). This match is important in moving the board and district forward and in maintaining good interpersonal relationships with board members. DuFour (2007) discusses the extent to which the superintendent's leadership style affects this match and the difficulty that can be encountered when board support of the superintendent changes.

Before going home, Richard read three more articles. The first was *The Ultimate Stress* (Sternberg, 2001). This article described crises faced by five superintendents and how they survived them. It provided an interesting perspective and food for thought about how Richard might approach his own situation if he decided to stay and fight the board president's request for his quiet departure.

The next two articles (Vasudeva, 2009; Hargreaves, 2009) addressed succession planning. These articles stressed the importance of being ready for leadership changes. Hargreaves notes that "few [leaders] want to step out of the limelight and give up the job, which makes the succession process difficult for the departing leader" (p. xx). Richard knew his board wanted leadership change, but he was not sure if they were ready for such change. He also knew that he would have to be very purposeful about stepping out of the limelight and making the superintendent search process as easy on those around him as he could.

Over the next few days, Richard talked extensively with his wife and assistant about the board president's request and possible next steps. He knew that whether or not he stayed, there would be a great deal of media attention and spin. He spoke to the executive directors of two state associations affiliated with school administrators and school boards to arrange professional development sessions on board governance for his board members.

Richard was not under the illusion that this professional development would magically fix his broken board and make them want to work with him again; rather, he felt strongly that he was obligated to try to help them become as successful as possible for the district, whether or not he was their superintendent. He also spoke to these association leaders regarding recommendations for attorneys specializing in superintendent departure issues should he need one as the process unfolded.

Richard took a half-day's vacation later that week, making time to read more articles on the topics of board/superintendent relations, unanticipated departures, and superintendent turnover. His hope was that these articles would shed further light on his plight. He wondered if he was the first and only superintendent to encounter this difficult situation, although he knew in his head and heart that he was not. This reality was confirmed as he read updates in local news sources and *Education Week* about various unanticipated departures of superintendents in districts. Regardless of the type or size of the district, no superintendent seemed to be immune from the possibility of an unanticipated departure.

Going to a university library had always been a source of comfort for Richard. As he searched for articles, his mind wandered back to the countless hours he had spent in libraries as an undergraduate and graduate student. He had never anticipated that he would one day return to the sanctuary of the library at such a critical juncture in his career.

Richard found six new articles of particular interest. Samuel (2011) and Borba (2010) focused on superintendent evaluations. Byrd, Drews, and Johnson (2006) and Fusarelli (2006) addressed the importance of board superintendent relations. Kamler (2011) described the role of search firms in superintendent selection. (This particular topic was quickly becoming more interesting and important to Richard as the days passed.) Finally, Cooper, Fusarelli, and Carella (2000) described what superintendents want and need in the position in order to find it rewarding and successful.

Superintendent evaluations had never been a very important area to Richard. He had always believed what his state association director had told him: "If the board is pleased, you can stay, and if the board isn't pleased, then they will find a reason for you to leave." In addition, Richard reflected on a talk he had attended from an expert in CEO evaluations in the health care field. The expert had stated: "I have seen CEOs with great formal evaluations pushed out the door and CEOs with marginal evaluations receive bonuses from the board of directors."

However, the more he reflected on the board's request to have him retire, the more he searched for answers to the question "Why?" He wondered whether he should have been more diligent about the evaluation process, and if he had been, whether it would have given him more indication about why the board wanted him to leave. He wondered whether he should adopt a different approach on superintendent evaluations so that in the event he sought and accepted another position, he might do things differently in this area to help ensure a better outcome than he was now experiencing.

Richard found Borba's article resonated with him as being very realistic. Borba described the evaluation process as one in which boards may be "well-intentioned and conscientious" but lack knowledge about how to evaluate a superintendent. Borba's writing also clearly captured the all-important political aspect of evaluating a superintendent, especially for board members who run on "anti–status quo" platforms.

The article by Samuel gave Richard grounds for reflection on his past ten-plus years as superintendent. Samuel reported on a survey of board members regarding the most critical areas boards used to evaluate superintendents and how these critical areas had changed in the past eight years. In 2002, Samuel found that boards were concerned about the critical areas of employee morale, student safety, and board/superintendent working relationships. The critical focus shifted in 2011 to student achievement and financial management. Richard reflected on his evaluations, professional development, and skill set. Had he kept current as trends changed? Perhaps not.

After taking a break at the Student Union and treating himself to an old college favorite snack of French fries and cherry walnut ice cream, Richard read the next articles about board/superintendent relations and superintendent turnover. Byrd, Drews, and Johnson provided an in-depth analysis of superintendent turnover from a historical perspective.

Historically, superintendents have been frustrated when boards involved themselves in issues outside the scope of their roles as the superintendent defined them. The terms "meddling" and "micromanaging" were used to describe these board involvements. Other critical factors that historically facilitated superintendent turnover were communication breakdowns between boards and superintendents and political issues that spun out of control. Interestingly, the level of district financial resources did not have a significant impact on the superintendent's tenure.

Richard gave careful thought to the survival analysis provided in the Byrd et al. article as it applied to his current situation. The three statistically significant factors (both positive and negative) that were shown to affect the superintendents' lengths of tenure were:

- A good working relationship with the board president
- Not being able to have a decision made at the board level
- Overall board/superintendent relations

Richard believed that when he compared his situation with these variables, he found they matched up remarkably well in a negative way.

Richard skimmed the next article on board/superintendent relations. Although not directly applicable to his situation, he found Fusarelli's 2006 case study of a nontraditional superintendent to be of interest. The case study was important because it reinforced the importance of a superintendent's interpersonal qualities, political savvy, and leadership skills when working with a board. Richard believed he was strong in each of these areas. Perhaps these strengths would help him depart with dignity and find an excellent new position elsewhere if he so chose.

As he thought of obtaining a new position, Richard next reviewed Kamler's article regarding the use of search firms. The study described how search firms had changed practices between 1995 and 2005. Kamler highlighted how during this time "massive retirements, increased expectations, and mounting political pressures have resulted in a diminished talent pool for school superintendents" (p. 115). Richard believed that the Kamler study confirmed his belief that the job had become increasingly difficult over his ten-year tenure.

As he enjoyed his final diet soda of the day at 4:30 p.m., Richard reviewed the article he had saved for last by Cooper et al. The article reported on an extensive survey study of superintendents based on a large sample size. The overall finding was that superintendents were proud of and satisfied with their own accomplishments but greatly concerned about the need to find new, talented leaders to take their places when they retired.

Although the article and the research contained within it were over ten years old, Richard found the survey results relevant when he considered what he desired as a superintendent: more support, clearer expectations, and better pay. In addition, superintendents ten years ago had wanted to move away from a strictly management function to a role that placed more emphasis on support and leadership. Richard's belief that people mattered was reaffirmed when he read that "people skills" were rated #1 by superintendents in a "skills needed" survey item.

As Richard finished his soda, he thought it would be helpful to summarize the articles in a readable, brief format for future reference. Perhaps he would take another half-day's vacation and reduce the major findings of the fifteen articles to a "quick review" format, a format that had always been helpful to his style of learning. This process also forced him to reflect and plan as he considered his next steps.

For now, however, dinner awaited. Tonight it would be salad and stir-fry. He would go to bed early and pray for strength to leave his current position with dignity to determine whether he should seek a new position or retire.

STUDY/DISCUSSION QUESTIONS

1. What are some of the reasons that you think Richard enjoyed success as superintendent for the first ten years of his tenure?
2. What did Richard notice that led him to believe that "he was being set up to fail"?
3. What could Richard have done to address board members who wanted to nonrenew the high school principal?
4. Do you think Richard should have considered his options to leave or retire from the district sooner? Why or why not?
5. Do you think Richard handled the technology referendum correctly? Why or why not? What might he have done differently to expend less personal "political capital"?
6. After reading chapters 5 and 6, does Richard's situation fit the Superintendent Experience Framework? If so, how? If not, why not?
7. After reading chapters 5 and 6, how many stages of the Unanticipated Departure Framework can you identify in Richard's scenario? Which stage is Richard experiencing at the end of the scenario? What advice would you have for Richard based on the key findings of the framework?

Chapter 3

RICHARD'S ARTICLE SUMMARY

Table 3.1

Article	Areas Covered	Major Findings

Stover, Del
 Walking the Line
 American School Board Journal,
 Vol. 198, No. 2,
 Feb. 2011
 pps. 17–20
	Board/superintendent partnership
	
	 Use of dashboard
		- Pay careful attention to the detail, structure, and communication of board/superintendent partnership
		 - Consider using a dashboard approach that outlines test scores, professional development, parent satisfaction, funding status, and more
		 - Do not bring controversial operational items to the board
		 - Boards should focus on
		  1. Planning for future
		  2. Evaluate how well district is doing in moving toward future

Kamler, E. Decade of Difference: 1995–2005 *Educational Administration Quarterly,* Vol. 45, No. 1, Feb. 2009, pps. 115–44	Search firm process How superintendent role has changed in ten years Succession planning	- "Massive retirements, increased expectations, and mounting political pressures have resulted in a diminished talent pool for school superintendents." - Focus on finding right superintendent match-up for boards
Samuel, C. Survey Detects Shifting Priorities of School Boards *Education Week,* Vol. 30, Issue 20 Feb. 9, 2011 Pps. 1, 22	Changes in the superintendent evaluation over an eight-year period Board/superintendent relations	- The importance of the board/superintendent relationship may be diminished compared to eight years ago - In 2002, the most critical areas used to evaluate superintendents were employee morale, student safety, board/superintendent working relationship - In 2010 the major evaluation areas were student achievement and financial management
Borba, A. L. The Superintendent's Evaluation: Bridging the Gap from Theory to Practice (online) Available: *http://www.aasa.org/con tent.aspx?id=12766,* 2010	Superintendent evaluation Using an outside facilitator	- Recognizes the complexity of serving on the board and believes most members are well-intentioned - Outside facilitator includes supt. and cost benefits of supt. in evaluation - Board must speak with "one voice and provide clear direction to the superintendent" - Supt. evaluation is difficult for boards - Supts. question the board's ability to conduct a fair and knowledgeable evaluation

Article	Areas Covered	Major Findings

Hargreaves, A. Leadership Succession and Sustainable Improvement *The School Administrator,* Dec. 2009 pps. 10–14	Succession planning	- Focus is primarily on principal training; however, can apply to Supts. interested in succession planning
		- Five challenges of succession planning are provided, including planning, management, emotional aspects, and not considering the entire system.
		- Four reasons for succession planning:
		  1. Increased leadership stability
		  2. Build systemic leadership
		  3. Develop distributed leadership
		  4. Create coaches for new leaders

Vasudeva, A. Training for Succession *The School Administrator,* Dec. 2009 pps. 16–19	Succession planning	- Under the direction of the Stanford University School of Education and School Redesign Network this article describes Mapleton Public School District (Colorado) succession planning program - A policy states "The superintendent shall not fail to protect the district from loss of its superintendent or other key staff" - Approximately 35 administrators were in initial phase of program which included mentoring and seminar support 25 remained in the program several years later and program advocates claimed success for the approach
Namit, C. Sharpening a District's Leadership Model *The School Administrator,* Dec. 2008 pps. 54–59	Governance model Superintendent evaluation	- Describes the two types of governance models districts typically use— traditional or policy - Most districts use traditional, which means boards are involved in a wide-range of functions and supts. are usually evaluated once or twice a year in a traditional model vs. ongoing evaluation in policy governance - Article promotes use of more continuous superintendent evaluation model which includes board self-assessment - Three tiers are considered for goal achievement—global, board, and superintendent/district

Article	Areas Covered	Major Findings
DuFour, R. In Praise of Top-Down Leadership *The School Administrator,* Nov. 2008 pps. 38–42	Leadership style	- Describes importance of Boards and superintendents being aware of superintendent leadership style - Three styles are autocratic, laissez-faire, and loose-tight - Each style has advantages with special emphasis on positives of using a loose-tight approach also called top-down - Board/superintendent match-ups are critical and each of the three leadership styles can encounter difficulty

Byrd, J., Drews, C., and Johnson, J.
Factors Impacting Superintendent Turnover: Lessons from the Field
National Council of the Professors of Educational Administrators (NCPEA), Education Leadership Review,
Vol. 7, No. 2,
2006
11 pages
	Superintendent turnover	- Authors studied 141 Texas superintendents in 2004-05—found average tenure was 5 years, district size not critical variable, 40% had doctorate
		- Major items related to instability of profession—superintendent/board communication and increased politics in profession
		- Found three factors may contribute to survival:
		  1. Work with board president
		  2. Be able to get decision from board
		  3. Improved board/superintendent relations
		- Must search for reasons why boards get so involved

Fusarelli, B. C. School Board and Superintendent Relations: Issues of Continuity, Conflict, and Community *Journal of Cases in Educational Leadership,* Vol. 9, No. 1, Mar. 2006 pps. 44–57	Turnover Nontraditional superintendents	- This district case study reports on a district where board/superintendent conflict occurred and the supt. was nontraditional (military background) - Authors believe education level of superintendent does not matter; rather, that superintendent has the interpersonal qualities, political savvy, and leadership skills - School governance and board role also reviewed

Article	Areas Covered	Major Findings
Kinsella, M. P. A School District's Search for a New Superintendent *Journal of School Leadership*, Vol. 14, May 2004 pps. 286–307	Search process Importance of match between board and superintendent	- The role of the search consultant as gatekeeper is described in this one-district case study - Issue of confidentiality and privacy are reviewed - Ultimately, the author believes that while credentials and achievements are important in a board's selection decision, the people-centered skills and how a perspective superintendent connects with the interviewing board is crucial
Sternberg, R. The Ultimate Stress *The School Administrator*, Sep. 2001	Departure/tenure	- As a newspaper journalist, Sternberg describes in detail the survival stories of five superintendents - Reasons for conflict included racial issues, school safety issue, budget crisis, "new" board seeking new leadership style, and challenge by a disgruntled job seeker.
Cooper, B. S., Fusarelli, L. D., &Carella, V. A. Career Crisis in the School Superintendency: The Results of a National Survey. *AASA, National Center for Education Statistics*, Washington, D.C. 2000, 51 pages	Tenure Leadership style What superintendents want	- Authors report on extensive survey of superintendents SPEAR— (Superintendents Professional Expectations and Advancement Review) - Found superintendents wanted more support, clearer expectations from board, and better pay - Superintendents believe people skills still #1 skill set needed, and expressed interest in moving to a more supportive, resource role from a strictly management role - Superintendents believed they made a positive difference
McAdams, R. A Systems Approach to School Reform *Phi Delta Kappa*, Vol. 79, No. 2, Oct. 1997 pps. 138–143	Board/superintendent relations Politics	- Board/superintendent power struggles are examined and author describes superintendent vulnerability to shifts in board membership - Superintendents can become victims to board "whimsical priorities and enthusiasm" - Describes answers for reducing board/superintendent conflicts, including having a clear vision and mission, addressing political issues, giving a supt. CEO status - There is a need for boards and supts. To understand the change process.

Article	Areas Covered	Major Findings

McCarthy, R. J. & Bennett, J. H. If You're Fired, Here's How to Land on Your Feet *Executive Educator*, Apr. 1991 pps. 14–17	Tenure
	
	Firing
		- This case study describes the painful, emotional aspects of the firing of a superintendent
		- The authors suggest specific steps a superintendent should follow if faced with termination:
		  1. Don't act in haste
		  2. Seek help from a counselor
		  3. Deal with your family
		  4. Contact a trusted colleague
		  5. Seek legal advice
		  6. Then meet with the board

Chapter Four

The Story of Randy J.

Randy sat back in his chair and smiled. He had just been offered the opportunity to teach a course at Central University on the superintendency, something he had always wanted to do. He looked through his calendar and blocked out Thursday evenings for twelve weeks during the spring term. He was pleased to note that there were no pressing conflicts. It was late in the day, and Randy had a few minutes to browse online through the book recommendations made by the department chair at Central. He ordered several books and looked forward to reviewing them.

This was Randy's second year at North Elm School District, located in a wealthy suburb of a large metropolitan area. He liked his new district, and so far, they seemed pleased with his leadership. He and the board had created a five-year strategic plan that was moving forward, and the community supported strong schools with facilities referendums and little opposition to standard taxation practices. The difficulties Randy faced in his new position were the types of difficulties that were part and parcel of the position. For the most part, differences, difficulties, and disagreements centered on issues, not people, and the overarching priority of the district was clearly centered on the students.

Randy was also pleased that after a difficult transition from his previous superintendency, his wife and children were adjusting well to their new home in North Elm. His wife, Jamie, was an accountant, and she was able to keep most of her clients through the move. His daughter, Emily, was in eighth grade and his son, Aiden, was a high school sophomore. Initially, they were very upset about leaving their home and friends in South Maple but were able to keep in contact through social networks and occasional weekend visits. They quickly made new friends at North Elm and were involved in a variety of school activities. All in all, North Elm was feeling like home.

Chapter 4

Aiden had a basketball game that evening, and Randy met Jamie and Emily at the gym. As he watched the game, his mind wandered to his last months at South Maple and how hard it had been for his family to deal with the stress of his position there. In hindsight, Randy was able to appreciate anew just how difficult it had been and how glad he was that he was able to obtain the superintendency at North Elm. The hurt and stress now largely behind him, he began to think that maybe teaching the course at Central University would give him an opportunity to reflect more objectively on the circumstances that had led to his departure from South Maple.

Over the next week, Randy found himself thinking more and more about his departure from South Maple. It had been his first superintendency, and at thirty-five, he was young and ambitious. He began teaching biology at age twenty-three and obtained his master's degree in education administration six years later. Randy was an assistant principal at West Cedar High School for three years before becoming the principal there. During his three years as principal, Randy worked on his doctorate in education administration through Central University, finishing his degree in the spring before he was hired as South Maple's superintendent. He had a reputation in the region for being an up-and-coming administrator whose professional yet personable demeanor complemented his talents for leadership and his knowledge of school district operations, policies, and politics. He was forward thinking about schools and curriculum, and his student-centered philosophy was apparent in his day-to-day interactions with students, staff, teachers, parents, and central office administrators.

His first five years at South Maple were successful ones. The previous superintendent had retired and stayed in the community, offering his help to make the transition a smooth one for Randy. Randy was able to confer with the retired superintendent, particularly during his first year at South Maple. The board worked well together and had a solid strategic plan in place that Randy was able to continue to execute during his first three years. There was one year of budget cuts, and he and the board worked through them well and were able to minimize the negative effects on the district.

In the spring of his third year, two new board members were elected, and they presented some challenges to Randy. They questioned many details of various initiatives that other board members previously had not. Over the next two years, Randy learned how to anticipate these board members' questions and provided more detailed information and scheduled extra workshops and informational meetings to address their concerns.

Through his diligence and his ability to listen and address the concerns of these board members, he was able to work with them. He understood that they, too, wanted what was best for students but often had objections to how the district wanted to achieve this goal. In the end, working with these board members resulted in better outcomes due to their questioning and the district's more careful review of the details surrounding issues, programs, and initiatives.

Randy was particularly pleased when he reached the five-year mark at South Maple. In that year, the district passed a building referendum, and construction was underway for a new elementary school in addition to significant updates to a middle school and the entire district technology infrastructure. He had a good relationship with community organizations and the local media, and the board was engaged in their own professional development that was very effective in helping new board members understand the roles and responsibilities of the board, education finance, and how boards can help facilitate student achievement.

Although the district was generally running smoothly, new challenges were emerging in the winter of Randy's sixth year as superintendent that reflected changes in the district's demographic composition and economic stability. The state board of education had recently issued an initial warning to the district because the records for suspensions and expulsions showed that far more students of color were suspended or expelled than white students during the past year. This problem of disproportionality in suspensions and expulsions was not uncommon throughout the state, but South Maple had a history of low expulsion rates, so had not been cited by the state up until this time.

As the population shifted in South Maple in the previous five years, more students were referred for suspensions and expulsions. The board, until last year, issued relatively few expulsions; however, with the addition of a new board member who ran on a platform of making the schools safer, more students were expelled than had been in previous years.

The warning from the state board of education was making the local news, and Randy had been compelled to give interviews to the local newspaper and appear on a local cable television show. He received several e-mails and phone calls from parents and community members on both sides of the issue. Some accused Randy and the district of being racist by expelling students of color and not white students. Others supported this new district practice, saying that they believed that the schools were now safer for their children.

The other two pressing issues facing the district involved the realities of economics. Due to changes in state funding and a generally weak economy, significant budget cuts loomed for the coming year. The board asked Randy to make a list of possible budget cuts that the board could review. Two budget cuts in particular created a great deal of media attention and political pressure on the board members and the administration. The first was a cut in the program for gifted and talented students and the second was a significant change in the district hockey program.

The gifted and talented program in the district had the support of very vocal parents who were highly involved in their schools' volunteering and fund-raising efforts. Although several other programs had experienced some cutbacks over the past five years, Randy had been hesitant to make cuts to the gifted and talented program because he knew it would be politically difficult. However, as he reviewed the budget with his administrative team for the coming year, he believed it was the right thing to do for the good of all students in the district that cuts in the gifted and talented program at least be considered by the board. As Randy suspected, when the proposed possible cuts became public, the political pushback from the parents and the media was immediate.

The parents of students involved in the hockey program and the coaches themselves were also very vocal interest groups in the district. The reality was that the hockey program cost far and away more per student than any other sport in the district. In addition, not all schools in the conference had a hockey team; that is, there was not the same expectation that the district should maintain a team in hockey the same way that there was an expectation that the district should maintain teams in basketball, football, track, and volleyball. Randy and his administrative team had put forth the suggestion that the district sponsor a club team, where parents would pay most of the costs of ice time and equipment. While the club team would not be under the umbrella of the state athletic association, it would have opportunities to play club teams from other communities and offer students a hockey experience without the district having to bear the cost.

Before the club team proposal was announced at a board meeting, one board member had already been in contact with a hockey parent, who had gone to the local media to draw attention to the issue. At the board meeting where the possible cuts would first be discussed, parents and the hockey coach were in attendance and spoke to the board during the citizen comments portion of the board meeting. Calls, e-mails, and blog posts to the district and in the local media were placing board members and the administration under significant pressure to maintain the hockey program as a district-funded sport sanctioned by the state athletic association.

All three of these challenges were coming at once and created a great deal of stress and many late nights for Randy. The board members were also feeling the pressure and needed his time and support more than ever. The board seemed divided in their support of Randy: Some board members were overall supportive that he had addressed political "sacred cows" in the budget, while other board members were upset that they were under such pressure to make unpopular cuts. However, to their credit, the board supported Randy as a group and made it clear to the media that they would be responsible for the ultimate vote; the superintendent had merely done what was asked of him by providing them with a list of those budget cuts that would, in his opinion, cause the least negative effects to student achievement in the district.

In the early spring, just as Randy was beginning to feel as though he was going to be able to bring these issues to resolution, a new and unexpected issue surfaced. Steve Erickson, the principal at South Maple High, announced that he was resigning to take a position as the director of instruction at North Elm. It was an excellent opportunity for Steve, but Randy was upset to see him leave. They had worked well together, and Steve's leadership had been exemplary.

When anyone walked into South Maple High, they knew they were someplace special. The climate and culture was warm and caring, yet full of excitement and energy. Steve had a talent for bringing faculty, staff, and students together using a combination of humor and seriousness that made others want to be like him. He knew the ins and outs of the building and everyone who made it work. He was truly a veteran captain at the helm of his ship. He would be difficult to replace.

When the applications for Steve's replacement started coming in, Randy was disconcerted to see that Ellen Steadman had submitted an application. Ellen was the middle school principal at South Maple East Middle School. She had been at East for four years and had done an adequate and acceptable, if uninspiring, job in the position. Randy believed she had talent for leadership, but she also still had a lot to learn.

Ellen's strengths were in her ability to network and communicate. She was very personable as well as being socially and politically savvy. As a lifelong resident of South Maple married to a prominent business owner in town, Ellen was a very popular principal with the parents and community members. The downside was that her strengths made her appear more competent than she actually was at many aspects of the job.

Ellen's background was in elementary education. She taught kindergarten and then fifth grade for ten years before becoming the middle school principal at East. She had struggled with curriculum and scheduling issues since becoming a middle school principal, and Randy was fairly certain that these struggles would be magnified at the high school level. In two separate emergency incidents in the past three years, Ellen had not followed the district crisis plan, and her overreactions created more chaos than reassurance. Finally, Ellen struggled with discipline issues at the middle school level. Preteens and teenagers were not kindergarten students, and Ellen had difficulty enforcing school policies fairly and effectively.

Randy did not want to grant Ellen an interview but knew that it was common protocol and courtesy to grant interviews to acting principals who were interested in transferring to another school. Against his better judgment, Randy called Ellen in for the first round of interviews. These interviews were conducted with a team of school personnel. Ellen impressed the school personnel team with her personable demeanor and answers that demonstrated her community-minded approach to leading a school. She advanced through the first round of interviews. The school team did not have the same information that Randy did about Ellen, and he did not feel comfortable sharing it with them.

Three candidates were chosen for the second round of interviews. Ellen was the only internal candidate. For this round of interviews, the superintendent and directors conducted the interviews, and the superintendent made the final decision about who to hire, pending the board's approval. Randy was beginning to feel a great deal of pressure from the board to hire Ellen as the new South Maple High principal, and he was feeling stuck. He did not want to discuss Ellen's shortcomings with the board in any great depth, for fear that they would want her removed from her position at East. While Ellen was not ready to become a high school principal, she was learning and growing in her role as a middle school principal, and Randy did not want to see her opportunities cut short in South Maple.

Randy also understood the political ramifications of not hiring Ellen. He knew that there were business interests and civic groups that might never forgive him. While this was just one issue in a recent hailstorm of challenges, he was beginning to feel as though he was collecting those kinds of weights that accumulate over time to make a superintendent ineffective. Randy could avoid the political fallout and hire Ellen as the South Maple High principal, but he already knew that he was not going to do that because it would be disastrous for both Ellen and South Maple High School.

During the weeks leading up to the hiring of the new high school principal, Randy had begun to look at job openings in other districts and thought about activating his file with the search firm that worked with the South Maple board when he had been hired. Although his family was well settled in South Maple, the increasing political pressures and media coverage were drawing unwanted attention to Jamie and the children. Randy casually mentioned taking a job in another district one rare evening that they were able to have dinner together at home. Jamie seemed eager and interested, while Aiden and Emily got very quiet. Randy quickly changed the subject, and knew that if he wanted to take another position, he would have the support of his wife and together they could make a move easier for the kids.

When Randy became superintendent, he had done so with the full knowledge that his position might not be a long-term one. He liked the South Maple community well enough but had maintained a certain detachment so that he could objectively assess the viability of his effectiveness as a district leader. He did not want to be one of those superintendents who stayed around too long, waiting for the board to ask him to resign. He and Jamie had purchased a modest home, with easy resale being a very important factor in their purchase decision. Randy also had a keen awareness of his own value and worth, and knew that if he were no longer a good fit at South Maple, he would be a good fit somewhere else.

As Randy sat at his desk wondering how to tell Ellen that he was going to offer the position to one of the other two candidates, the phone rang. The call was from Patrick White, who worked with the search firm that South Maple had used to hire him as superintendent. For a brief time six years ago, Randy and Patrick were on the phone with great regularity as he went through the application and interview process on the journey to being hired by the board. It was more than a little interesting that Patrick had called at a time when Randy was thinking about activating his file with them and perhaps looking for another position.

Patrick told Randy that he had been keeping up on the district issues in South Maple, and he saw that Randy was getting a lot of heat for many of the positions he was taking, particularly regarding budget issues. Randy briefly filled in Patrick on some of the other issues that were simmering. Patrick listened and suggested that Randy might be a good fit for a new position opening up in North Elm. Randy immediately perked up at the suggestion. South Maple was a nice, mid-sized, self-contained community that he and his family had enjoyed very much. North Elm, on the other hand, was a vibrant, wealthy suburb of a large metropolitan area. Both he and Jamie loved the city, and North Elm was simply an ideal location and community. A position as school superintendent in North Elm would certainly be considered a positive step forward in career advancement.

After a brief discussion, Randy told Patrick he would update and activate his file with the search firm and submit an application for the North Elm position pending approval from his wife. Randy felt a sense of excitement and eagerness to meet a new challenge as well as renewed strength to move forward and take care of the district business at hand.

While he had this renewed energy, he called Ellen in and gently but firmly told her that one of the other candidates was going to be offered the position. Ellen was visibly shaken but handled the news in a professional manner, asking what she could do to improve her chances of being hired the next time. Randy was proud of her for handling the rejection well and told her to continue her work on the operational and educational aspects of being a school leader to build her knowledge base. He acknowledged all of the positive things she brought to the interview and told her that they would continue to discuss ways she could improve as a school leader as her evaluations came up.

Over the next few weeks, things happened very quickly. Jamie was very excited about the prospect of moving to North Elm, and she and Randy spent as much time as they could with Aiden and Emily talking about what a move might mean and look like. Within a week of updating his file and submitting an application for the North Elm superintendency, Randy was called for an initial interview. He took a half-day vacation to go up to North Elm and interview, keeping very quiet about the process, even though he knew his candidacy would become public if he became one of the finalists. Randy was very excited about the prospect of being the superintendent in North Elm but was also realistic about his chances, and wanted to set the stage for another successful year in South Maple, if need be.

Randy continued to defend his budget cut suggestions and indicated that he would entirely understand if the board chose not to approve them. His job was to give them viable options for budget cuts, and he felt he had done that job fairly, efficiently, and ethically.

To address the disproportionality issue, he was working to approve a new program in cooperation with the local Boys' and Girls' Club that was researched and proposed by a teacher-leader working toward a master's degree in education administration. The community and media backlash on the hiring of an outsider for the position of principal at South Maple High was hard and quick, and Randy knew that a few select grudges would continue for a long time to come. He was ready to deal with that knowing that South Maple High was in the hands of the best leader that he could find.

Within three weeks, Randy was named one of the finalists for the position at North Elm. The fact that he had applied for the position would now become public. He called the board president and together they worked the plan for informing the rest of the board. When board members found out that Randy was a finalist for a position in another district, they were, by and large, very upset. Randy had always been able to work with his board, even through difficult issues and personality differences.

It quickly became clear that if Randy did not get the position at North Elm, his continued tenure at South Maple would be even more tumultuous than it had been. The board was split on their support of Randy. A few board members asked him privately if there was anything they could offer to get him to withdraw his application from North Elm; he respectfully indicated that there was not. A few other board members became increasingly difficult to work with, clearly looking ahead at and for the next superintendent of South Maple.

Randy was offered, and accepted, the superintendency at North Elm, and that is when the situation at South Maple became unbearable. The media became openly hostile and critical of many decisions made in the past five years, most notably the decisions to hire an outside principal at South Maple High and the recent budget cuts. Board members interviewed by the media were considerably less supportive than they had been in the past.

The most hurtful part of the process came when the board published a list of criteria for the new superintendent that they developed with the help of a national search firm. The media took this list and made direct comparisons to

Randy's superintendency. The list of qualities was portrayed as what was needed to "fix" all of the things that Randy was not—for example, sensitive to the diverse needs of students in academics and extracurricular activities, and willingness to cultivate talent within the district. They lambasted his push for a hockey club team and cuts in the gifted and talented program, and strongly criticized not hiring Ellen as the principal of South Maple High.

The months dragged on, and eventually South Maple hired a new superintendent. She was an up-and-coming student services director from a nearby district. Randy questioned whether she would be a good long-term fit for the district, but he kept quiet, understanding that it was their choice and their issue. The new superintendent was scheduled to begin on July 1 at the beginning of the fiscal year when superintendents traditionally start, but since she lived so close, she was very involved in the district two months before that time.

In the meantime, Randy was laying groundwork at North Elm for his new position there. May and June were grueling months, with the stress of wrapping up his work at South Maple in a hostile environment where he was quickly becoming all but invisible, except when someone was needed to blame. In addition, he was also getting his family ready for the move, and setting the stage for work at North Elm. By the time July 1 came, he felt that he and his family were running out of a burning building away from South Maple to North Elm.

It was a Saturday afternoon during Christmas break of his second year at North Elm, and Randy was in his office preparing for his spring term superintendency course. As Randy reviewed books for use in the course, he found that many were very useful to him personally as he reflected back on his time at South Maple and considered how best to move forward at North Elm.

The Superintendent's Fieldbook by Cambron-McCabe, Cunningham, James, and Koff (2005) is more of a reference book than a textbook, including information on seven different topic areas: (1) leadership, (2) governance, (3) standards and assessments, (4) race and class, (5) school principals, (6) collaboration, and (7) public engagement. He liked the organization and found the issues addressed in the seven chapters to be very insightful, but he was also somewhat surprised that school board issues and school finance were not addressed in more depth.

Randy found himself evaluating his performance at South Maple in each of these seven categories, and he was surprised at what he found. Randy began to realize that perhaps he needed to be more attuned to community groups and political issues—perhaps his somewhat formal, detached style needed to be examined if he was to experience better long-term success at North Elm.

Randy felt that *The Superintendent as CEO* by Hoyle, Bjork, Collier, and Glass worked together well with *The Superintendent's Fieldbook*, particularly because of the clear and detailed discussion of standards for superintendents, including the history and evolution of standards and licensure requirements. He was excited to find a resource that included an in-depth discussion of how the American Association of School Administrators (AASA) guidelines, National Council for the Accreditation of Teacher Education (NCATE) guidelines, and Interstate School Leader Licensure Consortium (ISLLC) standards had evolved to their current-day status. Other professional certification organization efforts were also referenced.

Randy found one summary statement in the book to be most helpful, and he planned to use it when he introduced standards in his courses. The authors state, "AASA, ISLLC, and NCATE licensure and program standards provide a powerful means not only of improving professional preparation but also of leveling the playing field for all those involved in the preparation enterprise"(p. 12). This idea of "leveling the playing field" by introducing standards was one that Randy was sure would evoke rich and thoughtful dialogue in class.

Next, Randy reviewed *Educational Administration: Concepts and Practices* (2012) by Lunenburg and Ornstein. Randy decided he would use parts of the text as a supplement in his upcoming class. He believed the information on administration and the thorough coverage of leadership skills, motivational theory, decision making, and communication was timely and relevant to anyone considering the superintendency.

Randy was especially impressed with the extensive chapters on school finance and organizational change. These were two issues that Randy wanted to focus on in his courses, and the detailed, comprehensive coverage of these two topics were outstanding. The chapter on organizational change addressed important issues related to the forces for change, resistance to change, and overcoming that resistance. The chapter on school finance provided in-depth information on funding sources for schools, school financing trends, school effectiveness and productivity, and financing school construction. Randy knew that these materials would help his students understand these issues critical to any successful superintendency.

Randy then read Thomas Kersten's book, *Stepping into Administration* (2010). Although this book appeared to be intended for an audience of first-year principals, Randy found that it had much to offer future superintendents. Randy was most taken by the eight strategies for rookie leaders. These were simple "nuggets" of advice that Randy had learned the hard way. He wished someone had given him a list such as this one when he had started out at South Maple. The eight strategies are:

- Handle mail well
- Manage electronic communication effectively
- Use social networking appropriately
- Recognize appropriate and inappropriate uses of e-mail
- Manage paper
- Create a year-long planning calendar
- Dedicate certain times of the day for particular activities
- Conduct more efficient and effective meetings

Randy decided that he was going to share this list with his class. What struck him most about this list was its currency. Randy avoided social networking and was extremely careful about his use of e-mail, but he understood from watching his staff and his own children that many issues lurked in these forms of communication.

The last book that Randy reviewed for use with his students was *What Every Rookie Superintendent Should Know: Surviving Year One* by Reeves (2006). Randy related to the month-by-month "playbook" for aspiring superintendents and thought that it would help the students better understand what the superintendency is really like. He thought this book balanced attention and awareness of self with the needs of the job and had him thinking about topics fundamental to the superintendency that he did not consciously think about too often.

Randy found that this book made him think about his legacy, both in South Maple and in North Elm. He did understand that the things he did in South Maple, especially regarding the high school principal and the budget, were the right things to do, and he believed that the district was better for it. He felt he had done a good job of placing the needs of the students and the schools ahead of the desires of the media and a small handful of community members, even when he knew that he was using precious political capital to do it.

The class preparation had an important collateral effect on Randy that surprised him. It made him reflect on his work from a perspective that he had not considered in the past and to feel better about what he had accomplished in South Maple and about what he could accomplish in North Elm. He allowed himself to dream about how he could make North Elm a better school district and about how his own career could flourish there.

Randy thought about what he might do differently in North Elm in order to be more successful than he had been in South Maple. He began to see the importance of becoming personally more vested in the community to enable him to better understand and address the concerns of the media and citizens who were lifelong residents. He realized the need to be aware of the nonpermanent nature of the superintendency, but he also began to see the need to balance that realization with an increased presence in the here and now. Randy also vowed to make more time for self-reflection and to think about what he had done and would do next in a given situation.

It had been a challenging final year in South Maple, but Randy felt fortunate that he and his family were settled in North Elm. He was grateful he had been able to secure a new position that would work well for him, and he was excited about the opportunity to serve the district. Time would tell whether he would continue to learn and grow as a school leader, but one thing he felt sure about: His calling was in education and he had no regrets about his career choice.

STUDY/DISCUSSION QUESTIONS

1. What factors contributed to Randy's success during his first five years as superintendent at South Maple School District?
2. Do you think Randy made the "correct" budget cuts? What, if anything, do you think he should have considered further before recommending cutting the hockey and gifted and talented programs?
3. Did Randy do an adequate job of addressing difficult issues at South Maple (disproportionality; not hiring internal candidate)? What might he have done to address these situations more effectively?
4. Do you think Randy left his position too soon? Did he suffer from "the grass is greener" syndrome, where a new job looks more appealing than staying to address the difficult issues in a current job?
5. What is your opinion about how Randy viewed his position, his family, and his investment in the community? Do you agree with Randy's overall approach to his position at South Maple?
6. After reading chapters 5 and 6, does Randy's situation fit the Superintendent Experience Framework? If so, how? If not, why not?
7. After reading chapters 5 and 6, identify all four stages of the Unanticipated Departure Framework in Randy's scenario. How much has Randy followed the advice of the Key Findings? Would you characterize Randy as a "resilient leader"? Why or why not?

RANDY'S BOOK REVIEW

N. Cambron-McCabe, L. L. Cunningham, J. Harvey, and R. H. Koff, *The Superintendent's Fieldbook* (2005)

The authors state *The Superintendent's Fieldbook* is more similar to a reference book than a textbook. They suggest using the various topics for seminar discussion in an independent versus sequential manner, if so desired. The book is organized into seven major chapters: (1) leadership, (2) governance, (3) standards and assessment, (4) race and class, (5) school principals, (6) collaboration, and (7) public engagement. Each chapter covers different and highly important topics. Each chapter is organized in generally the same way and contains an overview, three to four subsections devoted to in-depth descriptions/discussions of issues within the topic, and a concluding section on reflective practice.

Each of the three or four sections under the seven topical chapters includes commentary from the four authors in addition to guest authors. Each of the authors has extensive university teaching experience, and several also have government experience.

A common thread linking the authors is their extensive and critical leadership in the Danforth Foundation's Forum for the American School Superintendent. Cambron-McCabe served as coordinator of the forum and Cunningham, Harvey, and Koff were on the advisory board or had served as an officer.

The Danforth Forum started in 1992 and was a ten-year project serving 200 superintendents with an active group of approximately 50 superintendents meeting at least annually. Superintendents determined each agenda. The forum was designed as a "safe harbor" for professional development (p. 324). The superintendents represented urban, rural, and suburban districts with goal of 50 percent or more at-risk district representation. Finally, the forum superintendents were a diverse group, and the goal was a 60 percent representation of women or members of minority groups.

The authors believe the seven topic areas are those that superintendents must understand and address, and with which they must grapple. They highlight their belief on the relevance of each topic with a series of "must" statements for superintendents:

- You must lead.
- You must lead within a governance structure that is hardly ideal.
- You must understand standards and assessment.
- You must worry about race and class in your district and set out to close the achievement gap.
- You must develop your school's principals.
- You will have to learn how to collaborate.
- You must engage your community (pp. 14–16).

The concluding chapter is a departure from the practical and realistic descriptions of the various issues superintendents must address. This chapter is an attempt to address several issues under historical theoretical "images" including machine, political, psychic, and domination by comparing them to emerging "images"—culture, organism, brain, and flux/transformation. In addition, four leadership styles are discussed: prophet, therapist, coach, and poet. These archetypes and images provide an interesting framework from which to step back and consider larger issues of leadership style and societal "drivers."

J. R. Hoyle, G. Bjork, V. Collier, and T. E. Glass, *The Superintendent as CEO: Standards-Based Performance* (2004)

This book is one of the most complete resources for considering standards from an epistemological, model-based perspective. The authors describe the book as follows:

> [This book is] a scholarly and, we hope, friendly research and field-based curriculum for professional development seminars and retreats for superintendent preparation programs in higher education. Caught between the positivist approach to education, as reflected in high-stakes testing, the No Child Left Behind Act (NCLB), curriculum standards, proficiencies, and competencies, and the less measurable, perhaps more spiritual, constructivist view, we have chosen to blend concerns of standards-based performance with constructivist reflections on multiple ways of knowing and acting in the complex role of CEO superintendent and with ideals of spirituality and servant leadership to help prepare school district CEOs for the turbulent world of education. (p. x)

The first chapter addresses direction to be considered when training and certifying a "CEO superintendent," including superintendent preparation programs, licensure and relicensure, and professional development. The authors, with extensive superintendent and university experience, clearly define the standards and skills needed to be an "executive-level" school leader.

Preparation programs for superintendents are discussed as well as clear and detailed descriptions of how standards and licensure requirements came to be. In-depth narratives of how AASA guidelines, NCATE guidelines, and ISLLC standards evolved to their current-day status are included. Other professional certification organization efforts are also referenced.

The authors describe an "executive" superintendent and articulate what such a superintendent should know and be able to do:

- Formulate a written vision statement for a district.
- Understand global issues within a context of influences on schools in a democratic society.
- Promote teaching and learning.
- Empower others to high performance levels.
- Be a problem solver and decision maker.
- Respect diversity, assess district climate.

- Use a proven leadership approach.
- Be a passionate leader for equity.

Chapters 2 through 9 are devoted to the eight AASA standards. The eight standards are described within a context of theory and case studies, with discussion questions that lend themselves to a seminar-type classroom setting. The authors have devoted an entire chapter to each standard, providing excellent depth of information and illustrative examples. The eight standards and chapters are:

- Organizational culture
- Politics of school governance (includes in-depth review of school board issues)
- Communications and community relations
- Management of organization, operations, and resources (school finance included)
- Technical core of education
- Instructional management
- Human resources
- Values and ethics

The book concludes with an engaging and informative chapter on leadership performance evaluation. Detailed school board assessment models for superintendent evaluations are included with examples according to each of the eight standards. Sample superintendent evaluations are included, including templates for both written and interview-style evaluation formats.

F. C. Lunenburg and A. C. Ornenstein, *Educational Administration: Concepts and Practices,* 6th ed. (2012)

This book covers the standard areas of educational leadership, including curriculum, instruction, school finance, school law, board/superintendent relations, and personnel. Lunenburg and Ornstein provide in-depth coverage of organizational theory, structure, administrative theory and processes, and the structural framework of local, state, and federal government involvement in education. In addition, administrative theory, organizational structure and culture, motivation, leadership, and decision making are also covered in depth. In short, this book is a comprehensive leadership reference.

The book is organized into fifteen chapters, and each chapter includes a summary, key terms, discussion questions, and suggested readings. These sections are particularly useful for quick reference or for facilitating more in-depth discussions on various topics. In addition, the beginning of each chapter includes focusing questions that help orient the reader quickly to the material being presented in the chapter.

The chapter on government and education (pp. 209–63) is a good example of the topic coverage the book offers. The chapter covers government in education from the federal to the local levels. First, the federal government's historical and present roles in education are discussed, then the state governments' (and state agencies') roles in education are covered. Next, Lunenburg and Ornstein discuss the organization of school districts and the roles of local school boards and superintendents. Finally, central office staff and principals are discussed. Readers are able to conceptualize the entire educational system from a governmental lens and understand how each component of the educational system is affected by different governmental entities.

Readers searching for a no-nonsense, comprehensive view of school administration should consider this book. All aspects of school administration are described within a context of current cultural and economic realities. Readers at all levels of experience and position will find the direct and applied messages to be of assistance and to be thought provoking.

T. A. Kersten, *Stepping into Administration: How to Succeed in Making the Move* (2010)

Although Kersten's book is primarily intended for first-year principals, the book has much to offer future superintendents as well. One attribute of the book is the clear and extensive description of how and what teachers should do and think through when considering a career in educational administration. The book places emphasis on research that is focused on factors to be considered in an educational career. In addition, suggestions for fledgling administrators regarding specific strategies to enhance a career are included.

Two major factors that often determine the likelihood of administrative success receive special attention in the book: visibility and relationship building. Readers will have to extrapolate from the classroom/principal examples for each factor to the superintendent role, but the activity would likely be worth the time and effort. Kersten devotes significant attention to the areas of budget development and leading special education. Working knowledge in each of these areas is crucial for principals and/or superintendents if they are to successfully lead and thrive in their positions.

Perhaps the most immediately useful, applied, and practical section of this book is the final chapter, entitled "Working Smarter, Not Harder." A wide range of audiences could benefit from this "quick-read" section, including college students, rookie leaders, veteran leaders, and retired professionals. The eight strategies seem so obvious that an initial read leads one to think and ask, "Why didn't I develop such a list?"

R. Reeves, *What Every Rookie Superintendent Should Know: Surviving Year One* (2006)

Reeves's book is intended for new district leaders and is a practical narrative that walks readers through a year of the superintendency. The book begins with an introduction describing what every rookie superintendent should know. Included in this introduction are worthwhile and practical tips regarding board/superintendent relations, the change process, teacher negotiations, and guidelines for personal reflections on superintendent career development.

The next twelve chapters are devoted to an in-depth, month-by-month chronology with scenarios including various topics and issues rookie superintendents are likely to encounter each month. Each chapter is filled with helpful sections that not only include scenarios but also questions for reflection, summaries, and references (usually five to ten sources). A partial listing of topics/issues covered in three different months is shown below, and provides a sense of Reeves's writing and teaching emphasis:

August

- Setting goals
- Union relations
- Starting school year
- Presenting who you are to staff
- Administrative team meetings
- Being visible
- Timing for personnel changes

February

- Consider role of superintendent and board elections
- Clarify your mission and effect on change process
- Consider need for strategic plan

June

- Learn more about learning organizations and future of district
- Gather ideas on how to improve professional development
- Review and revise technology plan
- Learn more about employee transitions and planning

Examples of the various issues to be addressed month by month provide the reader with a realistic and in-depth sense of the all-consuming nature of the superintendency. New superintendents are often amazed at the number, frequency, and intensity of issues that are always surfacing or resurfacing. Reeves provides a realistic picture of the pacing and sequencing of the high-stakes issues a superintendent must manage and resolve. Reeves suggests that a person who likes the closure of a checklist may struggle adjusting to the demands of the superintendency, where some issues often seem to go on endlessly without any resolution in sight.

After the entire year has been reviewed, the following chapter focuses on an overview of the entire year and discusses planning for the next year. This chapter changes direction from the day-to-day management of the district to focus on longer-term dreams, vision, and direction. The central question "Will I make a difference to the district?" is raised within the context of a superintendent's legacy.

The final chapter is a brief five-page section that addresses board members and their role in the district. The section includes a self-rating section for board members. Included in the self-rating instrument are items such as superintendent hiring practices, effective boardsmanship tips, beliefs regarding characteristics of good board members, and a brief assessment scale regarding district excellence.

Chapter Five

Interview Process, Demographics, and Development of Frameworks

The best way to learn about superintendents' unanticipated departures is to tap the experiences of those who have been through it. Initially, we thought it might be a challenge to find these superintendents. Fortunately, superintendents typically maintain a network of colleagues throughout the states in which they serve. Even though superintendents are an "*n* of one" in their districts, their professional lives are very public, and the media often chronicle the difficulties of a superintendent, board, and/or district. Given the effective networking among superintendents and the public media access to district woes, finding superintendents who had experienced unanticipated departures was an all-too-easy task.

Twenty-two superintendents were interviewed for this book. These superintendents had a wide range of experiences and served in many different types of districts. For some of these superintendents, the unanticipated departure was quite recent, while for others it happened some time ago. Regardless of when or how it occurred, the memories were vivid.

Although the information in this chapter is admittedly a bit dry and technical of necessity in order to show what we did, it is important to note that throughout this process we were struck by the "humanness" of the stories that the superintendents shared. That is, these unanticipated departures generally occurred as a result of human emotion and interaction, regardless of content, context, or lofty ideals. That being said, most of our superintendents did their best to take the high road, wanting "to act responsibly and ethically, but to do so, they usually . . . [had] to persevere and improvise, often over long periods" (Badaracco, 2002, p. 42).

Our sample was not scientific; that is, we interviewed those superintendents we knew or those who were referred to us and who were willing to share their stories. Our goal was to find patterns among our superintendents, and as we analyzed the interviews, patterns did indeed emerge. The conclusions drawn as a result of this research are deductions based on twenty-two superintendents, mostly from the Midwest, whom we knew had experienced unanticipated departures and whom we invited to participate in the interview process.

We believe it is very plausible that the findings of this project will stand up to replication on a larger scale. We would welcome independent replication of this project in a setting with a more scientific sampling method.

WHAT WE DID AND HOW WE DID IT: AN OVERVIEW

Superintendent Participation

The first task was to compile a list of superintendents who had been through a difficult departure process. This list came from several diverse sources, including association directors, collegial contacts, and media articles. The list initially consisted of twelve individuals. As we spread word of our project, we quickly learned of other superintendents who had gone through unanticipated departures who might be willing to give interviews. It was not long before we had the twenty-two superintendents who were interviewed for this book.

Most of our interviews were invitees to whom we reached out and made the initial contact. In a few instances, someone who had heard about our project approached us and offered to grant an interview. Still others heard about our project and acted as third-party liaisons, contacting the potential interviewee and getting back to us with an okay to make the contact. We were very concerned about making sure we approached superintendents carefully, because we knew that asking them to talk about their departure experiences "on the record" was a lot to ask.

We contacted the superintendents formally by mail and followed up with a phone call (see appendix 1). The initial contact was important, especially for those superintendents who were hesitant to tell their story and for whom the departure process had been particularly difficult. Some individuals understandably needed some time to think about whether they wanted to grant an interview. The reasons for this hesitation were often both political and personal.

We assured superintendents that they would have anonymity and that they would be able to tell their own story in their own words. Most departures involved at least some nasty politics and formal separation agreements, including "nondisparagement" clauses that prevented either the school board or the superintendent from making disparaging comments about the other side. Given these circumstances, it was understandable that these superintendents would give careful consideration about these factors before granting an interview.

When all concerns were addressed and the superintendent was ready to give an interview, one was scheduled. Typically, the interviews were scheduled within two weeks of receiving final verbal consent from the superintendent. All but one of the superintendents who initially agreed to give an interview did so and met with us at the appointed time; only one superintendent had second thoughts and declined the interview at the last minute.

The Interview Process

Interviews were conducted either in person or by conference call, depending on the preference of the superintendent. Each interview lasted anywhere from about forty-five minutes to almost two hours. The stage was set for each superintendent by reading an introductory paragraph about the purpose of our study and the parameters for the session, which read as follows:

> We are researching the short-term and long-term responses superintendents have when they leave a position under less-than-ideal or preferred conditions. Your responses, which will be used anonymously along with the responses of approximately twenty other superintendents, will help us identify commonalities of experiences among those individuals who undergo a less-than-ideal departure process. We hope to identify the point at which superintendents recognize that departure is imminent and what happens between that time and the time of actual departure. In addition, we hope to identify techniques and strategies that have helped superintendents survive and thrive during and after such a departure. It is our hope that the information we obtain through these interviews can be helpful to other superintendents as they negotiate contracts, conduct daily operations, and eventually undergo a departure process (whether peaceful or rocky). Thank you for your time and willingness to participate in this interview.

This introductory paragraph was followed by several demographic questions to find out about the background of the superintendents and the district in which they experienced an unanticipated departure. Often, by the time the superintendents had provided the demographic information, they were ready to tell their story, and we let them do so. Our interview guide contained a list of questions that we wanted to have addressed by the end of the interview, and as those questions were answered in the superintendents' narratives, we would check them off the list, and asked the questions that were not addressed later in the interview (*see* Interview Guide in appendix 2).

As interviewers, we made an effort to interfere with the superintendents' initial narratives as little as possible. Occasionally, one of us would ask a quick clarifying question, but for the most part the superintendents told their stories freely. Typically, these initial narratives comprised about one-quarter to one-half of the interview time.

When preparing for the interviews, it was anticipated that superintendents might be hesitant to speak freely and that they might want or need several questions for guidance. That was simply not the case. The superintendents shared a wealth of information with almost no prompting whatsoever. Indeed, for many of the superintendents, there was a sense of relief to be able to share their story for the purposes of passing on the valuable learning they had acquired as a result of the departure process.

Following the initial narratives, several follow-up questions were asked that helped us understand and clarify any points of confusion. Then we asked the superintendents any questions in our interview guide that had not been addressed up to that point. As we discuss later, most superintendents in the initial narrative covered some of the questions in our guide, while other questions were rarely covered in the initial narrative.

Finally, each interview concluded by asking the superintendents if they had any final words of wisdom that they would like to share with someone else who might be going through an unanticipated departure. These final thoughts comprised some of the most powerful material in the interviews. These words of wisdom served to both summarize and illustrate deep convictions and learning that resulted from the unanticipated departure experience.

All of the superintendents were deeply affected by the unanticipated departure, and their words of wisdom, advice, and encouragement were given in a most positive "survive and thrive" context. There was a clear sense from this group that they wanted their experiences to be of value to others who may be in the same situation.

PURPOSE AND CONTENT OF INTERVIEW QUESTIONS

The Purpose of the Interviews

Going into this project, we were interested in researching the challenges and difficulties that are typically part of an unanticipated departure in a way that would be useful to current and aspiring superintendents. Much discussion, thought, and reflection went into framing the research, and started with: What did we want to know from the twenty-two superintendents who were interviewed? The answer was simple, yet complex: We wanted to know about their experiences with unanticipated departures from a practical, leadership, and managing-the-totality-of-the-situation perspective. We wanted to know what they knew that could help others recognize and manage an unanticipated departure.

Learning about the events leading up to the departure from the superintendents' perspectives was critical in order to understand the context surrounding their management of the departure process. When an unanticipated departure occurs, it is not uncommon that the local public hears about the events through the media, which are most often likely to focus on the board members' perspective of the events and their ability to gather information on the departure. The superintendent's perspective, if it is included in the coverage, is typically in the form of a sound bite or crafted statement and is most likely incomplete at best.

We wanted to know about *process* surrounding an unanticipated departure, and we wanted to know how superintendents could best survive through and thrive after being involved in this process. The goal of this project was to focus on key aspects of the departure and to provide some guidance based on research and experience about the best ways to negotiate the choppy waters of an unanticipated departure.

The Content of Interview Questions

The interview questions were designed to ensure that we learned as much about the superintendent, the school district, and the unanticipated departure from each superintendent as possible. We asked the superintendents about their education and experience, and about the district in which the unanticipated departure occurred.

Specific questions addressed the context and chronology of the unanticipated departure. We wanted to understand the superintendents' perspectives of the events leading up to the knowledge that departure was imminent and beyond. Listening to the stories being told, it was evident that many of the superintendents knew that they were in challenging circumstances well before an unanticipated departure was being considered. Questions and comments related to context and chronology surrounding the departure included the following items:

- Describe the context in which you became the superintendent of the departure district.
- Describe the events that led to your departure. Did you see it coming?
- When did you know it was time to go?
- Based on what you know now, would you have left earlier or differently in hindsight? Why or why not?

It was important to understand the practical, business-oriented considerations related to unanticipated departures as much as possible from the interviews. Specific techniques, strategies, and legal considerations were included in this category of interview questions. Interview questions related to practical considerations of departure included the following items:

- Did you hire an attorney as part of the departure process?
- What were the general financial conditions of your departure?
- Did you have an exit strategy when you recognized that departure was imminent?
- What strategies or techniques did you use to help you through the departure?
- How were you replaced?

The board had a significant role in most of the superintendents' unanticipated departures. For the most part, superintendents did not need to be prompted in order to go into great detail about their relationships with the board and the role they felt that the board played in the departure process. Nonetheless, we did include a specific question to prompt superintendents to talk specifically about the board's role in their departure, which was only asked in one or two interviews. The question simply read: "What was the board's role in your departure?"

Personal and emotional considerations were an extremely important aspect of the superintendent interviews. It was critical to find out exactly what difficulties the superintendents faced and what specific techniques they used to overcome, learn from, and thrive after these difficulties. The emotional components of the interviews were often the most difficult for the superintendents, and many of them recounted personal turmoil and stress on family and district employees who were near and dear to them. Personal/emotional questions and comments in the interview guide included the following items:

- Describe your immediate responses and long-term personal reactions to your departure.
- What effects did the departure process have on your health?
- What effects did the departure have on your family?
- What effects did the departure have on the district?
- Did you do anything to cope with additional stress during the departure?
- What did you do to recover/thrive after the departure?

Finally, it was important that the superintendents had ample opportunities to share advice, take-aways, and other wisdom that they accumulated as a result of undergoing the departure process. Although we asked specific questions about advice for others and strategies that worked well, some of the best insights we received often came at the end of the interview when we asked the last question: "Is there anything else that you would like to say?" Invariably, no matter how much excellent advice had been given throughout the interview, most superintendents added a final thought that comprises some of the most important material in the book. Advice questions in the interview guide included the following items:

- What exit strategies would you recommend based on your experiences?
- What advice would you give to aspiring and/or current superintendents regarding unanticipated departures?

The Evolution of Frameworks

We wanted to capture as much of the unanticipated departure experience process as possible in our interviews, with a particular focus from the time the superintendents suspected that they might be in a departure situation to the time that they actually left. As we developed the interview questions, it became apparent that in order to obtain the best information about this critical time period, it was important to gather information about the entirety of their experiences, at least in the departure district.

As the interviews started, we began to realize that it was important not only for the research but also for the superintendents to be able to give adequate context for their departures. That is, the superintendents were able to recount their experiences best by being able to tell their whole stories.

As we analyzed the interviews, the commonalities of experience lent themselves to two distinct frameworks, which we created and labeled to reflect the way we used them. The first is a framework based on the years of experience of the superintendent, *The Superintendent Experience Framework*. This framework uses the number of years a superintendent has been in his or her position to focus on the #1 reason that superintendents experience unanticipated departure: board/superintendent conflict.

The second framework is based on a crisis management model, titled *The Unanticipated Departure Framework*. This model focuses on the superintendent and his or her perspective, experiences, and management of the unanticipated departure process. A full discussion of each of these frameworks follows.

The Superintendent Experience Framework

One of the first patterns that emerged as the data were analyzed involved the commonalities among superintendents with similar levels of district leadership experience. This model was primarily developed when studying the specific issue of board conflict, if and how it contributed to the unanticipated departure. That is, superintendents with less than three years of leadership experience encountered different board issues than superintendents with four to nine years of experience, and both groups experienced different board issues than district leaders with ten or more years of experience as superintendents.

This framework was the most effective way that we found to explore the specific issue of board/superintendent conflict. We did not want this project to be focused necessarily on board/superintendent conflict, but the reality is that this conflict is responsible for the overwhelming majority of unanticipated superintendent departures.

The Unanticipated Departure Framework

The Unanticipated Departure Framework is similar in concept to the National Incident Management System (NIMS) framework used in crisis management by the Department of Education (DOE) and many school districts throughout the country. In the crisis management model, the four phases are: (1) preparedness, (2) prevention and mitigation, (3) response, and (4) recovery (http://www.rem4ed.com/terms/terms.html). The superintendents we interviewed underwent their own personal crisis management, and we developed a four-phase model similar to the crisis management model to use as a framework to consider these processes: (1) preparation, (2) recognition, (3) management, (4) recovery and reflection. The four phases in the Unanticipated Departure Framework are described below:

- Preparation: the events and circumstances leading up to and surrounding the unanticipated departure
- Recognition: identifying the moment when the superintendents realized that it might be time to leave and the time between this identification and the actual departure
- Management: how the superintendent worked through the departure with the district, family, and friends
- Recovery and reflection: how the superintendent moved forward after the experience, and the reflections, hindsight, insights, and advice superintendents had for others

Significant shifts in outcome expectations and goal focuses occur, distinctly marking each phase in the unanticipated departure process as different from the other phases. In addition, the characteristics of each phase distinguish the departure process as different from other problems or issues to be solved or worked through.

Perhaps this model evolved as the natural result of having the superintendents tell their stories chronologically. Each story contained a before, during, and after piece of the unanticipated departure that, in some manner, covered all four phases of the process. However, it was not merely this chronological organization that was responsible for the four-phase model; shifts in orientation and action marked each phase and became clear in interview after interview.

This four-phase framework approach is important because it enabled us to organize parts of the process associated with preparation, recognition, management, and recovery and reflection in a way that can be identified as sound practice and good advice for current and aspiring superintendents. This point brings us to the ultimate purpose of this book, simply stated: to help current and aspiring superintendents navigate an unanticipated departure should they face one.

A detailed description of each of the four phases of the Unanticipated Departure Framework follows. Included in the description of the each stage are the key focus points of each phase and the interview questions that were answered in a way that helped the stage to emerge.

Preparation

Key focus points in preparation:

- Managing personal finances.
- Creating mind-set for leaving, if necessary.

The way that superintendents frame the permanency of their role and prepare for possible departure is an important aspect of managing an unanticipated departure well. How the superintendents managed personal finances and housing, how entrenched they become in the community, and how prepared they were to leave when the circumstances dictated were important preparation pieces. To this end, we found that many superintendents did understand that such a departure was a possibility when they accepted the position and took deliberate actions to ensure that they were positioned to handle such an event to the best of their ability.

The questions that superintendents answered by focusing on the preparation phase of departure included the following:

- What was the context in which you became the superintendent in this particular school district?
- What were the circumstances leading up to your departure from the superintendency?

Recognition

Key focus points in recognition:

- Decision to fight or leave must be made.
- Assessments might be necessary to determine whether a departure situation exists.
- Recognition is marked by a significant change in focus from the district to the departure.

One of the most important focuses of this project was to identify the moment when each superintendent realized that he or she might be in a situation that could result in an unanticipated departure. We believe that the time period starting with this recognition through the management process was the most critical period of the unanticipated departure. Whether this realization was a sudden epiphany or whether it came about gradually over time, the interview included many questions directed at identifying the moment when the superintendent realized that an unanticipated departure was probably imminent. These questions included the following:

- Did you see the unanticipated departure coming? If so, what were the signs?
- When did you know that an unanticipated departure was imminent?
- Did you have an exit strategy at the time you realized that departure was imminent?
- What was your immediate response when you recognized that departure was imminent?
- How long did you stay on as superintendent after this realization, and why?

Simply put, one of the keys to successfully working through an unanticipated departure is to realize and acknowledge that such a departure is very likely imminent. Sometimes, the board members realize that they want new leadership before the superintendent realizes it, and sometimes the superintendent understands that new leadership is needed before the board does. In still other instances, the board and superintendent come to the mutual realization that the match between the superintendent and the district is no longer compatible at about the same time, and that a change of leadership is perhaps the best solution.

Superintendents are trained to be problem solvers and to meet difficult situations head on. It can be very challenging for superintendents to realize and acknowledge that they may be in a situation that results in their own departure as part of the resolution. Such realization and acknowledgment requires either a great deal of objectivity or a direct message from someone else to that effect, such as a board member, family member, or colleague. However it occurs, there are emotional issues and practical process issues that must be attended to once the superintendent recognizes that he or she is in a departure situation.

Whether the realization that they are no longer wanted as leaders is one that superintendents come to on their own or whether someone else delivers the message, it can be a difficult pill to swallow, to say the least. It can shake the confidence and leadership ability of superintendents more than they might realize and can affect all aspects of leadership, effectively making the superintendent a "lame duck" in many instances.

This moment of realization and acknowledgment is a key element to working through an unanticipated departure, because once this moment has occurred, everything changes. A significant paradigm shift occurs where the goal for the superintendent and board becomes working out an exit strategy that is agreeable to all parties. The actions that occur once the paradigm has shifted through the realization that an unanticipated departure is imminent begins the next phase of the departure process.

Management

Key focus points in management:

- Looking out for both personal and district interests during the process of leaving.
- Negotiating a complete, legal, and equitable separation agreement with the district.
- Building and/or utilizing personal support systems.
- Leaving in the most professional manner possible; leaving the district in "good health."

When a superintendent leaves under unanticipated circumstances, it has a significant impact on the district and community. Simply put, it can be devastating if poorly managed. That is, the climate, culture, and circumstances of the district should continue to be well supported and sustained throughout the departure process. Superintendents typically also need to manage issues related to how the departure affects their family. Last, but certainly not least, superintendents need to move forward with their career as positively as possible.

Arguably, the most important learning from this project comes from discovering exactly what these superintendents did to manage their departures. That is, we have the advantage of their experience (251 years' worth) to help determine what actions, attitudes, and outlooks worked well in managing the departure, as well as pitfalls to avoid. We asked several questions about the actual departure process, including:

- How did you manage the district and what specific strategies did you use during the departure process?
- How did you manage your career/personal life and what specific strategies did you use during the departure process?
- What exit strategies would you recommend based on your experience?
- Did you retain legal counsel during the process?

In addition, superintendents were also asked about how they managed their personal reactions to the departure process, including:

- Did you seek the advice of friends, family, clergy, or a professional source?
- Did you have any health issues?
- Did you do anything specific to cope with the stress?

The management of the departure occurs when the superintendent is typically in the thick of the situation. This period can be very short, lasting mere weeks, or it can be drawn out over months, and sometimes even a year or more. The superintendents interviewed for this project described a wide variety of situations and approaches to management that reflect as many different approaches to departure as there are leadership styles among individuals. That being said, commonalities of experience can be described and documented to a relatively high degree.

Managing the unanticipated departure with professionalism and strength is no easy task, especially when a superintendent must also deal with the personal, emotional, often gut-wrenching component that is part and parcel of the unanticipated departure. Knowing and using appropriate resources, knowing and managing personal strengths and weaknesses, and thinking and acting with clear, purposeful direction are skills that the superintendents in this project discussed with the deep insight and conviction that comes with experience and commitment. Their insight and learning about both the professional and personal effects of the departure process illustrate the importance of quality leadership in all aspects of the superintendency—especially during an unanticipated departure.

Recovery and Reflection

Key focus points in recovery and reflection:

- Leave completely; avoid temptation to follow district news.

- Find another position as soon as possible if the career plan includes continued service as a superintendent.
- Take time to recover and reflect; find the new normal.

As with most things in life, there is life after. This axiom holds true when considering unanticipated departures from the superintendency. All superintendents interviewed for this project have moved on with their lives in meaningful ways that reflect overall personal and professional success.

That does not mean that recovery was easy for all; it wasn't. That does not mean some do not still harbor resentment; some do. The physical, mental, and emotional toll of such a process is very real; however, there was positive growth and learning, and many superintendents came to realize over time that the departure was ultimately a good thing for them and for their careers.

In addition to moving on after the departure, the superintendents interviewed also took time for reflection and shared their learning from the experience. There was a sense from most that they took whatever value they could from the experience and emerged the wiser from it. The questions in which superintendents focused on recovery and reflection in their responses included the following:

- What did you do to thrive after the departure?
- How were you replaced?
- Based on what you know now, would you have left later, earlier, or differently? Why or why not?
- What advice would you give to aspiring or current superintendents regarding such departures?

Recovery and reflection, like the rest of the stages of departure, are processes that require time and thoughtful working through. The superintendents interviewed shared their triumphs, trials, and tribulations reclaiming normalcy in their lives, and reestablishing successful career paths while thriving with family, friends, and colleagues. Overall, the unanticipated departure experiences reaffirmed what was important in their lives. They all had outstanding advice that they were willing to share to help other superintendents manage all stages of a possible unanticipated departure (see appendix 3).

SUPERINTENDENT SAMPLE AND DEMOGRAPHICS

We made every effort to obtain a diverse and representative sample of superintendents for this project. The American Association of School Administrators (AASA) data were used as post hoc comparison to determine how closely the sample mirrored national statistics (http://www.aasa.org/content.aspx?id=740). In many ways, the sample demographic statistics reflect the proportionalities of the statistics provided by the AASA. Table 5.1 provides the AASA demographics data and the project sample data.

Table 5.1

	Project (2011)		AASA (2006)
	Number (*n*)	Percentage (%)	
GENDER			
Male	14	64%	64%
Female	8	36%	36%
ETHNICITY			
White	20	91%	94%
Other	2	9%	6%
GEOGRAPHY			
Midwest	19	86%	N/A
South/East	3	14%	N/A
DISTRICT SIZE			
<1000	8	36%	47%
1,001 – 9,999	10	46%	46%
>10,000	4	18%	6%
DOCTORATE	15	68%	60%

Distinct similarities are apparent when comparing the AASA data and the project data, particularly the distribution according to gender, ethnicity, district size, and education. In terms of gender distribution, both the AASA and project data contained samples that were 64 percent men and 36 percent women. In terms of ethnicity, the AASA reports that about 6 percent of the nation's superintendents represent nonwhite ethnicities, while 9 percent of the project population represented nonwhite ethnicities. In terms of district size, the project sample represented slightly larger large-district (over 10,000 students) superintendents than AASA (18 percent versus 6 percent) and slightly fewer small-district (less than 1,000) superintendents (36 percent versus 47 percent). Both samples contained the same proportion of mid-size districts at 46 percent.

In terms of education, the project sample was represented by doctorate degrees slightly more often than the AASA population (68 percent versus 60 percent). In the project sample, the doctorates were primarily EdD degrees in the areas of educational leadership or educational administration. Most of the superintendents interviewed earned their doctorate degrees while working full time as a superintendent.

The project sample differed from national averages in some important ways, namely geographic representation and the age of superintendents. In terms of geographic representation, most of the project superintendents served schools in the Midwest (about 86 percent). Three of the superintendents (about 14 percent) served districts in other regions of the country. In terms of age, the AASA indicates that the mean age for superintendents is between fifty-four and fifty-five years of age. Our sample population was slightly older, with over half (about 55 percent) of the sample aged sixty to sixty-nine years when interviewed, although many of them served in the departure district during their fifties.

It is worth noting that the time between the unanticipated departure and the interview varied greatly among respondents. Table 5.2 illustrates the number of years between the unanticipated departure and the time the interview was given for the project sample.

Table 5.2

Years Since Unanticipated Departure	Number of Superintendents	Percentage
0 – 2 Years	9	41%
3 – 5 Years	6	27%
More than 5 Years	7	32%
Total	22	100%

The largest group of the superintendents (41 percent) interviewed for this project had experienced their unanticipated departure two or less years since the interview ($n = 9$). Most of these superintendents were removed from the experience by one position or career change. About 27 percent of the superintendents interviewed had undergone their unanticipated departures three to five years before the interview ($n = 6$), and 32 percent of superintendents experienced their unanticipated departure more than five years before the interview ($n = 7$). Some of these respondents were several positions removed from their unanticipated departure and/or had retired from the superintendency.

Experience of Superintendents

The superintendents interviewed for this book represent an impressive level of experience in education, leadership, and the superintendency. The twenty-two superintendents interviewed served a total of forty-three superintendencies and logged in 251 years of service, with an average length of total service per superintendent (although not in one superintendency) being 11.4 years (table 5.3). Of the 251 total years served as superintendents, 172 of those years were served in a district where the unanticipated departure occurred, with the average length of service in the departure district being 7.8 years, well above the average of 5 to 6 years indicated by AASA (table 5.4).

Table 5.3

Total Number of Supts.	Total # of Supt. Positions Held	Total Years of Supt. Service	Average Length of Service per Supt.
22	43	251	11.4 years

Table 5.4

Total Number of Supts.	Supt. Ending in Unanticipated Departure	Years of Service in Departure Position	Average Length of Service per Supt. in Departure District
22	22	172	7.8 years

These statistics indicate (and the information in the interviews confirms) that superintendents had success in other superintendencies before and after an unanticipated departure. We found that these superintendents were committed to making each district in which they served the best it could possibly be.

It is important, too, to acknowledge the many years of teaching and administrative service represented by the superintendents interviewed (table 5.5). The superintendents interviewed had over 250 combined years of teaching experience, and over 150 years combined in school administration, either as school principals or central office administrators.

Table 5.5

Number	Total Years as Classroom Teacher	Total Years as School Principal	Central Office Administration (non-Superintendent)	Total Years in Other Leadership Position
22	266			
16		87		
8			60	
6				38

When the years of teaching and administrative experience are added to the years of superintendent experience, the group of superintendents interviewed had over 650 years of combined experience in education, or an average of over 30 years of experience per individual. To say that this group brought a wealth of experience in education to their roles as superintendents is an understatement.

These demographic statistics are interesting for review but are presented with a significant caveat. The population was not chosen by a specific technique. For those of you who are research purists, our sampling techniques and size will no doubt fall woefully short; however, we were not in search of a particular subset or distribution of superintendents. We went in search of superintendents who had stories to tell about unanticipated departures, and we used various means to get them, including news stories, personal contacts, and association leads. We used a personalized approach, which yielded powerful and compelling stories that resulted in the development of the Superintendent Experience Framework, the Unanticipated Departure Framework, and many, many valuable lessons about navigating an unanticipated departure.

Chapter Six

Lessons Learned Using the Superintendent Experience and Unanticipated Departure Frameworks

The superintendents interviewed for this book provided a wealth of valuable information. This information was embedded in their stories and given as advice and "takeaways." In this chapter, we focus on this information using two frameworks. The first framework, the *Superintendent Experience Framework*, involves studying superintendents with varying levels of experience to examine the ways that new superintendents may experience unanticipated departures differently from more experienced superintendents. The second framework, the *Unanticipated Departure Framework*, is the four stages of the unanticipated departure process identified in the previous chapter (preparation, recognition, management, recovery and reflection).

Each superintendent's experiences with unanticipated departures were different; however, common themes and commonalities of experience emerged as the stories were told. The interview process provided superintendents with an opportunity to share their insights and learning as they reflected on their experiences. These insights provided important lessons and considerations for current and future superintendents as reflected using each of the two frameworks.

FRAMEWORK I: SUPERINTENDENT EXPERIENCE FRAMEWORK

As we analyzed and discussed the data, an interesting trend clearly emerged. There appears to be a strong association between certain reasons for unanticipated departure and the number of years that a superintendent has served as a superintendent that resulted in an unanticipated departure. Table 6.1 summarizes the findings, which show consistent reasons for unanticipated departure in each group, broadly categorized by years of service as a superintendent relative to the unanticipated departure.

Table 6.1

Number in Group	Years of Experience in Departed District	Reason(s) for Departure
Group 1 ($n= 7$)	3 years or less	Each of seven (100%) departed due to conflict with Board of Education early in the superintendency
Group 2 ($n = 6$)	4 to 9 years	Four of six (67%) left for reasons not related to board conflict, reasons varied greatly
Group 3 ($n = 9$)	10 years to 23 years	Each of nine (100%) departed as result of a conflict with one or two board members that evolved over a several year period, eventually, board votes of 6-1 or 5-2 turned against the superintendent to 3-4, 2-5, 1-6

Perhaps the most interesting aspect of considering unanticipated departures of a superintendent by years of service is that a bimodal distribution appears to exist regarding the relationship between the board and the superintendent. Superintendents serving three years or less and those serving for ten years or more experienced unanticipated departure entirely due to board/superintendent conflict, while over half of those superintendents serving four to nine years left for other reasons.

Less Than Three Years of Experience as Superintendent

Interestingly, the nature of the board/superintendent conflict with newer superintendents is very different from the nature of this conflict with experienced superintendents, and enough commonalities within the inexperienced superintendent group and the highly experienced superintendent group were found that are worth discussing in depth.

As might be expected, the inexperienced superintendents often chose positions that were not a good initial fit for their strengths, abilities, and skill sets, which led to a different type of problem set than those experienced by superintendents with more years on the job. Experienced superintendents, on the other hand, were well suited to their positions for a long time, and typically experienced board members who were ready for change.

Seven of the superintendents interviewed had served as a superintendent for three years or less before experiencing an unanticipated departure. The interviews revealed that these less-experienced superintendents encountered a very early onset of board member resistance that created challenges almost from the beginning of the superintendent's tenure.

Upon reflection, these superintendents indicated that either they, their families, or their close friends had cautioned them against taking the position; however, for many, it was their first superintendency, and high-level educational leadership can be a difficult field to break into—it is simply hard to say "no" to a job offer. Beyond that, many inexperienced superintendents (and experienced ones also) believe that they can have a positive impact in virtually any setting or situation. What is initially viewed as a manageable challenge simply becomes more than they bargained for.

For the most part, these superintendents underestimated the difficulties presented by the positions they accepted. Simply stated, these superintendents were not ready for the challenges, questions, and unrest presented by their boards. Early challenges by one or two board members turned quickly into a majority of opposition to each superintendent. It was time to leave almost as each superintendent was getting himself or herself established. The honeymoon period, if any, was very brief!

Ten or More Years of Experience as Superintendent

By contrast, superintendents serving ten years or more had very different conflicts with their boards that eventually ended in departure. These board/superintendent relationships were well established, strong, and productive for many years, and typically either eroded over time or eroded very suddenly, depending on the nature of the board.

In situations where the board relationships eroded over time, board opposition took place with gradual board turnover, until the board that originally hired the superintendent was completely replaced. These "new" board members were not vested in the superintendent the way the original hiring board was, and the superintendent became a much more vulnerable target for any issue that became contested. Often, there was a sense the new board wanted an opportunity to choose a new leader and run things their way, not under the leadership of someone hired by the "old" board.

When board support eroded gradually, it was not always obvious that support was eroding since a specific issue or event did not trigger it. Superintendents described their awareness as a sudden sense of realization after a number of years that "things had changed—the board support was thin or gone." At first, most superintendents did not read into negative votes an opposition to the superintendent, but over time, the string of negative votes in opposition to the superintendent was sending a clear message.

Where the board relationships eroded more suddenly, the election of one or two oppositional board members became the catalyst for the unanticipated superintendent departure quickly. The new board members created a climate of suspicion and distrust between the board and superintendent by swaying others on the board with minor oppositional tendencies. That is, these highly oppositional board members empowered other board members to join them "against" the superintendent.

Where one or two highly oppositional board members quickly eroded board support for the superintendent, they simply decided that it was time for new leadership. That is, they did not bother to wait for an issue or problem that would lend itself to a change in leadership. As the challenges became more persistent, typically over a period of less than one year, votes that had been 6–1 or 5–2 in support of the superintendent's recommendations in the past became 4–3, 3–4, or 2–5, regardless of the issue or initiative.

Many of the superintendents with ten or more years of experience longed to serve board members of the original board that hired them. They were proud of the important work accomplished by these boards and felt that, as a team, the board and administration worked to make the district a better place for student learning.

When the oppositional boards were established, this group of experienced superintendents felt unappreciated, outdated, angry, and resistant to the "new" board. Yet these superintendents stated that they worked diligently trying to establish a healthy working relationship with these boards. They had developed many effective strategies for working with oppositional board members and instituted these strategies in attempts to strengthen the board/superintendent relationship. However, these tried-and-true strategies were no longer effective with their oppositional boards.

Four to Nine Years of Experience as Superintendent

The superintendents who anticipated an early departure between four and nine years were a most interesting and disparate group. Of the six, two experienced board conflict similar to those superintendents serving less than three years. The other four left for very different and highly individual reasons:

- One was offered a job unexpectedly in the private sector with a significant salary and benefit increase.
- One left believing it was time. She/he had run the course in that job and had developed lots of "rocks in the pockets" advocating for students in the district.

- One left to try to help a community heal through new leadership, which was necessary due to a significant community divide over a district issue in which the superintendent was not directly involved.
- One left due to mental and physical health demands of the superintendency and switched professions by going for advanced graduate training in a brand new field.

Those superintendents with four to nine years of experience overall took a broader perspective and were not so consumed by the job that they were unable to see the possibilities beyond the challenges in front of them. That is, there appeared be more balance of power between the board and the superintendent among this group than among the other two groups, which could likely be why there were fewer departures based on board conflict in this group than in the other two groups.

The superintendents in this group also had the benefit of experience and a sense of their own value in relationship to the organization. This view helped to balance their relationship with the board. These superintendents knew that if they were not finding a high degree of career satisfaction in their current roles, they were in a good position to find a better fit elsewhere, whether or not that fit was as a superintendent. These superintendents perceived a high degree of choice regarding their next career move, and some exercised that choice.

It is interesting to note that, using Malcolm Gladwell's (2008) observations in *Outliers*, a person gains a recognizable level of expertise after about 10,000 hours of engaging in the practice or activity. Superintendents typically reach the 10,000-hour mark somewhere between the fourth and fifth year of their service as superintendent. This phenomenon may be reflected in these superintendents who had competence and confidence to assess whether they wanted to continue in their current role or seek a new and different challenge, sometimes in district leadership and sometimes moving to other professions as indicated above.

Analyzing the interviews using the *Superintendent Experience Framework* revealed that superintendents involved in an unanticipated departure encountered board conflict at each of three experience levels: less than three years, four to nine years, and ten or more years. The board/superintendent relationship dynamics and issues that led to the superintendent departure were very different for each group.

There is no doubt that the board most likely plays a pivotal role in any unanticipated departure. Whether the departure is initiated by the board, a few board members, or the superintendent cannot be predicted with full accuracy; however, it is interesting to be aware that the tendencies for board conflict can and do change depending on the number of years the superintendent has been serving.

It seems that the most obvious and striking lesson learned from organizing the superintendent interviews according to this framework is that there are pitfalls to the superintendency, regardless of how long one serves in the position. That is, if a superintendent initially gets into a district that is a good fit and meets the challenges presented to him or her, that does not mean that the troubles are over—far from it. District issues, continued risk of board conflict, and other career options are possible challenges that a superintendent with mid-level experience can face. A highly experienced superintendent still runs the risk of board conflict from board members who are ready for new leadership and want to pick a new leader, which is the most powerful exercise of duty for any school board.

There appears to be a cycle of leadership, and it would be of value to study this phenomenon in further depth.

Vignettes for Further Study

The following vignettes provide brief narratives of three individuals who have served as superintendents. These stories are representative of our twenty-two interviews, and each represents a different period of time in the superintendency. Superintendent W is new to the position, having served three years, and Superintendent C is slightly more experienced, having served for four years. Superintendent M is an example of an experienced superintendent, having served for more than ten years. These vignettes provide brief yet compelling stories of unanticipated departures and convey messages and meanings beyond data and trends.

The stories are composite sketches of the twenty-two superintendent interviews and represent the commonalities shared among superintendents by experience group. The stories have been heavily disguised and combined to protect the identities of the superintendents. All of the vignettes are based on actual events as reported to us in the interviews.

Superintendent W: Less Than Three Years of Experience

Superintendent W brought a lifetime of dedication serving students to his first superintendency, which lasted three years. He had a comprehensive teaching background that included service in a wide range of settings, from rural districts to the nation's largest districts. He believed his classroom experience and various positions held across the country made him well suited for his first superintendency, which was in a small rural district located in a remote part of the state.

Before his first superintendency, W served as a leader for approximately seven years in a private marketing firm. However, his heart was always in education, and he returned to public education and served as principal in rural and suburban settings before obtaining his first position as a superintendent.

Because of W's strong sense of commitment and confidence, he stayed in his first superintendency after his informal advisors, consisting of his wife and friends, believed he should have left after the first year. W experienced numerous board conflicts and he perceived that the board was engaged in micromanaging. Upon reflection, W realized that he was "mentally leaving" as soon as he started; however, he had internal conflicts about walking away from the district's challenges, holding onto the belief that "I can work with anyone and make anything work."

Two major challenges in the district increased board conflict in years 2 and 3 of W's tenure as superintendent, escalating an already difficult working relationship between W and his board. The first challenge was financial. The district never had a robust general fund, and under the previous superintendent the board had voted to spend much of what little there was on new programs and school improvements. Now, the district sometimes had to borrow in order to meet payroll and bills during certain months of the year. The media had publicized the amount of interest the district was paying when it had to borrow, leaving the board open to intense criticism from the community.

The other major challenge during year 3 was the board's increased micromanagement, specifically their involvement in hiring decisions that should have been made by the superintendent. W perceived that the board was micromanaging and he felt that they were working around him and not with him.

Although he was not happy with the situation, W was working with it as best he could until he learned that the board had directly hired a school principal without his involvement. When W found out what the board had done, he was mortified and embarrassed. It was only then that he clearly understood what little leadership influence he had with the board, and he knew that the only solution for him was to move on.

After three extremely difficult years in his first position as superintendent, W left and found a different superintendency in a larger district, which was very satisfying. He described his new position as a great experience, noting that he was a good match with the board. The emotional recovery from his first superintendency is an ongoing process that continues to this day.

Superintendent C: Four to Nine Years of Experience

Superintendent C entered the superintendency in what he described as a nontraditional manner. Prior to returning to college to become certified as a teacher, Superintendent C worked in both the private and public sectors as a leader. He found his ultimate mission always included commitment to public education.

His years as a teacher were very enjoyable and he quickly advanced through the administrative ranks, landing a superintendency at a relatively young age. C viewed his first superintendency as a transition to another superintendency. As a result, C consciously avoided establishing deep family or community roots, knowing that he would likely move his family on to another position in a relatively short period of time.

This view was reinforced when during, his third and fourth years, he encountered major political resistance, but interestingly, not from the board of education. This resistance came from a politically motivated group of employees and led Superintendent C to seek another, "better" superintendency.

Since he had begun as superintendent, there had been a small but vocal group of these employees who simply did not like him. They did not like the fact that he was young and that his leadership style was very different from the prior superintendent. C had made several attempts to reach out to this group but to no avail. The board support that C enjoyed only seemed to make things worse with this group of employees.

C understood that this kind of resistance was part and parcel of the superintendency and did his best to work with this group of employees. Despite his efforts, these employees made their dislike of C evident in public places; they regularly made scenes in public, treating C with an embarrassing lack of civility and crudeness. They sent letters to the editor and called the local radio talk show. They showed up at sporting events and other district-sponsored functions and were constantly criticizing C in voices loud enough for all around to hear.

Things came to a head when a teacher-advisor was caught redirecting funds from a club account for other uses. This teacher had used several thousand dollars from the club account in the past two years to buy unauthorized supplies for her chemistry classroom. These supplies were in no way attached to the club activities, and in fact, when she had requested these particular supplies from the district, the request had been denied.

The employees who did not like C unanimously supported the teacher, even though the teacher had redirected funds and had purchased unauthorized materials that the district had specifically refused to fund. This employee group used media outlets and their own network to spin the story in attempts to place blame on the administration.

Over the coming weeks, the district became very divided over this teacher and the misuse of funds. The pressure and attempts to blame the administration and superintendent continued to mount. C believed that this event was a signal it was time to put his plan to find another position into action, even though it was sooner than he had hoped. He sensed that the district would not fully recover from this incident and the underlying animosity attached to his leadership until he was gone.

When C had accepted his first superintendency, he had laid the foundation for his next position by purchasing a modestly priced home, preparing his family, building his résumé, and maintaining a forward-thinking mindset. When the time came to act, C was prepared and was able to focus on the job search and the interview process. He was able to get a position that was a good fit in a community that his family enjoys. Superintendent C is thoroughly enjoying his new position, which he describes as vibrant and challenging.

Superintendent M: More Than Ten Years of Experience

Superintendent M enjoyed being a superintendent and believed the position clearly fit with her lifelong mission of service as a K–12 educator. This mission, combined with faith and friends, provided her with the foundation to successfully endure a rocky departure with a "new board" near the time she planned to retire after well over ten years of service to the district as superintendent.

To this date, Superintendent M believes the unanticipated departure was unavoidable based on the direction and drive of several new board members. As candidates, these board members ran campaign platforms centered on the need to change the status quo, including the superintendent. When these new board members were elected, they wasted no time in putting their plan into action.

However, removing M from the superintendency proved to be more challenging than these board members had anticipated. It was, as she recounts, "death by a thousand cuts." M enjoyed a great deal of community and employee support, and she had been responsible for implementing many successful new initiatives in the district. In addition, new school buildings and major renovations to old buildings had been successfully funded through referendum during her tenure in the district.

M wanted to retire on her own terms and felt that she deserved that much in recognition of her years of service in the district. It was not to be. After about fourteen months, the new board members finally succeeded in wearing M down and she agreed to retire early with a generous severance package negotiated by her attorney. In exchange, she left the district immediately and quietly, with no formal retirement "send-off."

M rebounded from the sudden departure and credits her faith, friends, and grounded lifestyle for her strength and recovery. Superintendent M's advice to other superintendents is to approach unanticipated departures as more likely to occur than not. M believes superintendents need to count the votes on the board and determine in a realistic way how long to fight board opposition if support for administrative action is consistently lacking. These considerations must be made while carefully weighing the impact of engaging the board in battles within the district and community.

FRAMEWORK II: FOUR STAGES OF UNANTICIPATED DEPARTURE

The twenty-two superintendents interviewed generated eighty-seven individual pieces of advice covering many aspects of unanticipated superintendent departure. This advice and the accompanying stories were studied from many different angles and ultimately resulted in both the Superintendent Experience Framework and the Unanticipated Departure Framework. In an intermediary step before the above frameworks were finalized, these pieces of advice were analyzed and organized into seven categories:

1. Determining your attitude
2. Considerations before taking a job
3. Specific guidelines and issues related to departure
4. Assessing/reassessing reality and relationships
5. Personal/health considerations
6. Legal/professional issues
7. Succession planning

The full list of advice under each category above can be found in appendix 3. These categories of advice were all eventually incorporated into the *Unanticipated Departure Framework* and appear as key findings and lessons. A total of twenty-five key findings were identified in the final framework, with many of the individual pieces of advice being condensed and combined where appropriate. This framework is a starting point and intended to be built upon and enriched as we learn more about the procedures, politics, dynamics, and emotions surrounding superintendent unanticipated departure from the perspective of the superintendent experiencing the departure.

Something that became interesting as we continued to analyze the data was the similarity between the advice that superintendents gave regarding unanticipated departure and the set of characteristics of resilient leaders. Allison (2012) identified six practices demonstrated by resilient leaders, and the advice given by our superintendents reflects these six practices in many ways, which becomes evident as the *Unanticipated Departure Framework* results are discussed in detail:

1. Engage in personal renewal.
2. Watch your mouth.
3. Stay optimistic.
4. Quickly blunt the impact of setbacks.
5. Cultivate networks before challenges hit.
6. See patterns; use insights for change.

These practices of resilient leaders were also practices for successful unanticipated departure, and there is a broad parallel between the two reflected in the seven categories that we initially identified above and the key findings and lessons learned in the *Unanticipated Departure Framework*.

Preparation

Key Findings in the Preparation Phase

- Purchase modest housing; do not overtax your budget.
- Budget for an attorney should you need one.
- Anticipate a departure from the first day; realize you are replaceable.
- Study the district you are going to serve in depth before you accept the job.
- Listen to any "gut feelings" you have about this position not being a good fit.
- Keep an open mind regarding next career moves.

It is never too early to begin planning for the possibility of an unanticipated departure, and it can start as early as the interview process. Here, the old adage "an ounce of prevention is worth a pound of cure" applies. While the board is interviewing the superintendent candidate, the candidate should also be interviewing the board and assessing whether the district is a good fit for his or her abilities and values.

Some of the superintendents interviewed indicated that they felt reservations about the position from which they experienced the unanticipated departure even during the hiring process. As one superintendent stated, "It was bad from the get-go; a little voice said don't take the job." Sometimes, friends, family, or colleagues sense the superintendent's hesitation and reservation and may voice concerns; the superintendents in hindsight overall wished they had paid more attention when those concerns were voiced.

Several superintendents stressed the importance of studying the district in depth before being hired. Some of the superintendents interviewed were extremely diligent about researching a district before taking a position, while others wished they had been. It is not enough merely to research the district, but to do so with as realistic a perspective as possible. Are the issues in the district something that can be addressed by effective leadership? Several superintendents indicated that they would not take a position where they believed they were either being set up to fail or where the problems that the board wanted addressed could not be effectively addressed in the ways that the board wanted.

Presuming the fit with the district seems like a good one, there are still ways to prepare in the event that an unanticipated departure occurs. There is a saying among superintendents that you should have your bags packed under your desk, because the dynamics of the position can change quickly and superintendent turnover is prevalent.

Key Lessons around Preparation

Several superintendents stated emphatically the importance of planning a departure from the first day. These superintendents understood from the start that some issues and problems arise in a district that are not solvable and may require (often from the board's perspective) a change in leadership. Other superintendents did not plan for departure early and instead dug in and tried to fix problems that could not be fixed, no matter what they did. It was only after months or years of struggle that the realization that they needed to leave became apparent.

Managing housing costs is a key to this preparation. If an unanticipated departure occurs, it will often require that the superintendent move, whether it has been planned for or not. Some of the superintendents interviewed indicated that they purposely purchased modest homes where they served. Such a home gave them peace of mind and the knowledge that an unanticipated move would not result in financial hardship. A modest home is often easier to sell in the event of a move, and if it does not sell quickly, managing payments while obtaining housing elsewhere is not financially debilitating.

Several of the superintendents interviewed had been (or were currently) in the position of having two (and even three!) homes to maintain while waiting for the home in the departure district to sell. These superintendents wished they had obtained more modest housing in the departure districts. For these superintendents, the housing piece highlighted the transitional nature of the superintendency and the importance of not getting too comfortable in a position or community.

Managing personal finances extends to having funds set aside should the need to hire an attorney arise. Several superintendents interviewed hired their own personal attorneys to help them negotiate the specific terms of their departures and to ensure that they were leaving in a legal and ethical manner. There is no question that an unanticipated departure is a high-stakes proposition and may come at a time for the superintendent when future employment is still uncertain. Budgeting in advance for adequate personal representation can bring peace of mind knowing that a professional support system can be put in place should the need arise.

A final piece of advice told through the experiences of superintendents was to keep an open mind regarding career direction. The reality is that the superintendency is not for everyone, and it is hard to know for sure until it is experienced. In addition, once a person has been a superintendent, the possibility of other career options may become available. Knowing that there are good personal career choices can help to prepare for the possibility of an unanticipated departure.

Many superintendents we interviewed stressed the importance of preparation and anticipation of the possibility that an unanticipated departure may occur, regardless of how long a person has served or how well the district seemed to be running at any given time. Most of the preparation was designed to ensure that the superintendents were able to take care of themselves and their families no matter what happened in the district.

It is worth noting that these superintendents used this preparation approach, whether or not the superintendency they served ended in an unanticipated departure. Of the forty-three superintendencies served by the twenty-two superintendents interviewed, twenty superintendencies either had a smooth termination, a retirement, or are still active. That is, the preparation brought peace of mind and did not contribute to their departure. Rather, their preparation for a possible departure enabled them to do their jobs more effectively. Preparation for the possibility of departure made many superintendents more careful about the positions they chose to accept and made them aware that the connections to community they were making were not necessarily going to be long term.

Recognition

Key Findings in the Recognition Phase

- There are several ways recognition of an unanticipated departure can occur: slowly over time, quickly with a shift in personnel (usually board members), or unexpectedly.
- The decision regarding whether to fight or leave is a difficult one.

- The reasons for the departure are typically not personally about you; political issues, and others' personal agendas are at play.
- It is important to reassess realities and relationships as part of the recognition phase to determine whether you are truly in a departure situation.
- Assess personal health and well-being to help determine whether you are in a departure situation.
- Initiate discussion with your board as soon as possible once you recognize that you may be in a departure situation.
- Avoid "the road of despair" as you make your assessments and determinations.

Recognition is a critical moment when the superintendent realizes that an unanticipated departure is likely or imminent. This recognition can come suddenly as a surprise or can build gradually until a moment in time when a tipping point is reached. However it happens, it is a moment after which everything changes. The paradigm shifts from a framework where the superintendent is part of the district fabric to one where the superintendent recognizes that he or she will soon not be.

The superintendents we interviewed came to recognize that they were in a departure situation in many different ways. The most common occurrence was a shift in the board that eventually resulted in eroded support. As one superintendent stated, "You need to count votes. I had 5–2 support for most issues, then 4–3, and eventually 3–4. I knew they didn't want me there anymore." Once support eroded, it was a short time, usually measured in weeks or months, before the superintendent was removed. The moment of recognition occurred for these superintendents when they realized that board support for superintendent-led initiatives and advice had shifted to an oppositional majority.

Sometimes, the erosion of board support is the result of a sudden change, either the loss or addition of a pivotal and/or influential board member. Some regular board turnover is normal, but when that turnover results in the loss of a key supporter or the addition of a key resistor, it can have terminal effects on the superintendent's tenure in the district. In some instances, these new resistant board members strengthened the resistant positions of other board members who had been more neutral in the past.

In a few instances, some board members became what the superintendents perceived as micromanaging and intrusive. Board members evidenced this micromanaging by personally overseeing district initiatives and projects, going unannounced to schools, meeting directly with principals, and even spending significant time in the district office overseeing various operations. These actions resulted in conflicts about role and eventually resulted in the superintendent's departure.

In situations where the fit was not good from the beginning, there is a slightly different dynamic at play. These superintendents talked about their belief that they could make things better if they just tried harder or stayed longer hours or could figure out how to please the board. As one superintendent said, "I kept telling myself I could make this better, but I couldn't. It was so hard to admit that I couldn't, because that would mean admitting failure." In these instances, evidence that an unanticipated departure is imminent is apparent for some time, and it is the superintendent's ability to acknowledge it that moves the departure process forward.

> The amount of time JZ was spending at school was overwhelming him. He was expected to be working at all times of the day and night. There were late-night board meetings, which sometimes did not end until after midnight. There were also other regularly scheduled evening events that JZ was expected to attend. The sheer time expectation and no time for any personal interests simply became too much. . . .There was nothing that JZ could do to win the board's approval.

In still another common scenario, an issue or crisis in the district spins out of control and the board/community looks for someone to blame. Sometimes, special interest groups, such as parents or teachers' unions, create these issues, and other times they are part and parcel of school management, such as a personnel issue or budgeting item.

Finally, a small number of superintendents were simply blindsided by a request from the board to leave. In some cases, some underlying tension was building, but the superintendent did not realize that it was serious enough for the board to ask the superintendent to leave. In other cases, the superintendents had absolutely no reason to expect or believe that the board wanted them to resign. Nothing in superintendent evaluations, action plans, or implementations gave these superintendents any indication that there were any unsolvable problems. One day, the board president simply came and asked for a resignation. These unexpected resignation requests are particularly chilling, because these superintendents had absolutely no opportunity to be part of the decision-making process.

> DN was a highly regarded superintendent. She received glowing reviews from her board and served on various statewide committees. Imagine DN's surprise when she was called by the board president one Sunday and told to leave the district and never return. She left with no district recognition or acknowledgment for her more than twenty years of service.

Key Lessons around Recognition

Recognizing that a potential departure situation exists has many direct effects on a superintendent and his or her ability to be of meaningful service in the position. The first decision (if it is not already made) is whether to fight for the position. Our superintendents acknowledged that this decision is a difficult one. They suggested talking to colleagues outside of the district and even seeking psychological help if necessary. Most importantly, to the extent possible, many superintendents talked at length about keeping personal emotions at bay and working hard to get a realistic assessment of what the board or others in the district are thinking and planning for the superintendency.

Lessons about managing personal emotions during this recognition process were very practical and centered on efforts to understand that issues surrounding unanticipated departures are most likely not purely personal. Reminding oneself that superintendent tenures are notoriously unstable and not necessarily a reflection of a person's worth or underlying ability is important to managing the emotional turmoil that is inherent in this process. Looking at all facets of the superintendency, including the political nature of the role and the agendas of others, can help place natural emotional reactions that go along with recognizing that departure may be imminent in the context of a larger framework.

The recognition phase is a time when it is critically important to step back and reassess personal perceptions of relationships and realities. A superintendent may simply not be a good match, whether the match was never good from the beginning or whether personnel turnover has occurred on the board or in key district/community positions. Reassessing relationships to determine the accuracy of superintendent's perceptions and working to fully understand how the departure scenario is unfolding is an important part of recognition that will help in the management phase of the departure.

Taking note of personal health and well-being was also a key to determining whether a departure situation exists. Several superintendents noted that increasing stress and the onset of health issues were important signs that the district climate and working relationships with the board and key stakeholders were no longer healthy and reaching a critical juncture. Sometimes, when relationships erode over time and stress continues to steadily increase, it can be a challenge to recognize that a tipping point has actually occurred.

> AW described the problem board member as a professional stalker. This highly educated and verbal board member would challenge every decision and recommendation on minute levels of detail. When the board member started, the board vote was 6–1 in support of most superintendent recommendations. Over a period of several years, the vote gradually changed to 4–3, then to 3–4 against most superintendent recommendations. AW's health suffered. Her doctor told her that the increased levels of stress were negatively affecting her

blood pressure and blood sugar. This buildup of stress and health decline continued until one day AW finally realized and understood that the board no longer wanted her to lead the district.

Another important lesson learned was about initiating discussion if possible, especially with the board. Communication is critical when determining whether a departure situation truly exists, and sometimes lack of communication can be a strong indication of the seriousness of the situation. Whether or not the issues rise to the level of a superintendent departure, creating and/or maintaining the best lines of communication possible can help assess the seriousness of the issues and the implications for the superintendent and the district. Attempting to maintain the status quo after a superintendent suspects or recognizes that more serious underlying issues exist can make the departure process or nondeparture resolution much more difficult.

> HM noticed that communication had changed significantly with the board. There was a lot of it, but it wasn't necessarily productive. Board meetings were running late into the night/early into the morning, with members often perseverating and straying away from the agenda. Board members were questioning items that were once routine or passed on the consent agenda, without any forewarning to the superintendent. The board president started to ask for a great deal of information, and little was actually used in decision-making processes. Several board members began to spend more time in the district and asking questions of HM at all hours, calling, texting, and e-mailing. Lastly, the media's coverage of the district was shifting. More negative than positive stories were being published and the blogs were merciless. In short, HM experienced lots of communication, but it was all negative and unproductive. He was beginning to get the message.

Lastly, many superintendents caution against going down the "road of despair." This lesson goes to managing personal emotions during this time. It is when situations are most difficult that a leader must be at the top of his or her game in order to achieve the best possible outcomes, both individually and for the district. Letting feelings of victimization and hopelessness cloud judgment and action can negatively affect these outcomes.

> DA left the district unexpectedly as the result of a scandal in which he was made the scapegoat. Instead of succumbing to feelings of victimization, which would have been very normal, he framed his situation in terms of the health of the district. That is, DA believed in order for the district to heal, they needed to start fresh with new leadership.

Negative feelings are entirely normal and natural; however, they should be addressed. Assembling a support system—whether it is family, friends, trusted colleagues, church connections, or trained professionals—can help feelings of isolation, despair, and failure. Assembling this support system is a key aspect of recognizing that a departure situation exists and preparing for the next phase of departure, management.

> TM had served in the district for three years and left her friends from her hometown to take the position. During the months leading up to her unanticipated departure when board relations were strained and stress levels were high, TM spent many weekends in her hometown, relying on her friends, civic activities, and church affiliations to step back, gain perspective, and regroup for the coming week, and ultimately, the departure.

Management

Key Findings in the Management Phase

- The management phase is about formalizing all terms of your departure in a clear agreement between you and the district.
- Consider hiring an attorney to ensure a complete, legal, and equitable agreement is reached that fairly represents your interests.
- Leave the district as healthy as possible. Tend to community building and operations until your last day.
- Offer support and leadership to staff who will likely be under increased stress, uncertainty, and tension as a result of your departure.
- Avoid becoming isolated; stay engaged in your position and seek out emotional support from appropriate sources.
- You cannot change the board; this phase is about departure, not about fixing problems.
- Make a clean break from the district and possibly from the community.

After recognizing that an unanticipated departure potentially exists, a shift in the superintendency occurs from a focus on managing the district to a focus on managing the departure process. In most unanticipated departure scenarios, the departure occurs before the current superintendent's contract runs out. How long should the current superintendent stay? What are the plans for replacing the superintendent? How does one negotiate out of a contract with the board? These are practical issues that need to be addressed in the management phase of the unanticipated departure, along with many other, often emotional, issues.

As with other aspects of unanticipated departures, there are no "one-size-fits-all" answers to these questions or one "correct" way of managing the departure. The process for departure is dependent on several factors, including who initiated the departure, whether the superintendent has other employment plans, and the degree of contention between the superintendent and board or other key stakeholders.

It is not uncommon for the superintendent to hire a personal attorney during the departure process. Sometimes, board/superintendent relationships are so eroded that the board and superintendent simply cannot meet face-to-face to work out the terms of the departure. Other times, the board and superintendent are still on speaking terms, and the attorney is hired to make sure that the terms of the departure are complete, legal, and equitable for the superintendent. That is, some superintendents hired an attorney for extensive board negotiations, while others hired an attorney merely to review the separation agreement to ensure that it reflected what was actually agreed upon.

The negotiated terms of the departure, including salary and benefit extensions, varied significantly among the superintendents interviewed. A few superintendents who had already secured new employment and had personal financial security did not want to add extra financial burden to the district with a large buyout. These superintendents recognized that a departure situation was imminent and proactively sought another position to manage the departure. Legally, these individuals were likely entitled to larger settlements than they ultimately agreed to in the interest of leaving the district as healthy as possible and with as many good feelings as possible.

Other superintendents were forced out by the board or by other internal or external groups through the board. These superintendents typically negotiated a buyout package that provided them with financial stability for a time while they figured out next career steps. This negotiation typically not only included the financial terms of the departure but also the timing for the departure. Often, these agreements also included nondisparagement clauses whereby each party agrees that they will not bad-mouth the other in public. These clauses are not meant to quash transparency; rather, they are intended to prevent personal mudslinging that would only harm individuals and the district to no productive end.

The issue of superintendent replacement was discussed in several interviews. Sometimes, the board wanted the departing superintendent to help in the hiring or to make recommendations for an interim or replacement superintendent. Those who did help regretted it. Most of the superintendents interviewed indicated that they declined to be involved in any aspect of hiring their successor. They believed it was important to make a clean break and let the board decide what they needed in a new leader.

Along with these professional considerations, managing an unanticipated departure has significant implications on family and other aspects of personal life. Many superintendents talked at length about how hard the process was on their families. Often, the departure was public; reading about it in the newspaper and hearing about it in the community was emotionally very difficult on family members. That being said, many of our superintendents also talked at length about the incredible support that family offered, particularly a spouse or a close relative. That is, the stories that were told over and over were stories of families coming together and becoming even more strongly bonded, even though the process was extremely difficult.

Personally managing the stress of the departure was another important factor that was discussed at length by most superintendents. Some sought counseling from various sources and benefited from it. Although a few did eat or drink somewhat more during the departure process (as might be expected), many became more conscious about following healthy maintenance routines, including exercising and eating well. They sensed that they needed to be both physically and mentally at their best in order to make the right decisions throughout the departure process, and whatever self-discipline and/or self-care routines they used, these were increased during the departure process.

> JG served a large district, and his jaw hit the ground one evening when he received a call saying that one of his board members had commandeered a district snowplow for use in a local parade. The plow had the district logo clearly painted on all sides, and it rolled down the road shooting sparks as the blade hit the pavement and the board member waved from the driver's seat. JG went home and fixed a strong drink, telling his wife that his days in the district were numbered. Indeed they were. Finding some relief from the fallout in a few extra drinks were part of the coping mechanism JG used over the next several weeks.

Key Lessons around Management

Most of the superintendents interviewed recommended hiring an attorney to help them work through the departure process. Typically, attorneys became involved when the details of separations were being worked out between boards and superintendents. In addition to helping with the financial negotiations (including extended salary and benefits), the attorneys also helped to negotiate the timing of the departure and any nondisparagement clauses that were included in the agreement.

Many superintendents also stressed the importance of trying to find another position before leaving the current position. Many referred to this approach as "getting back on the horse" as soon as possible. While one superintendent indicated that this approach specifically did not work for him, most agreed that this approach helped them move on successfully from the departure district.

> FW was devastated by his unanticipated departure. He was terrified about going out and interviewing for another position. A longtime family friend, knowing FW's talent and love of education and leadership, helped FW get over his fear by suggesting positions, and at one point, driving FW to an

interview and kicking him out of the car. FW is a very successful district administrator today and credits his friend for helping him "get back on the horse."

In some instances, other districts sought out replacements through public postings or search firms when the news of an imminent departure became public. Other superintendents actively began seeking positions and were able to secure employment before or shortly after the departure. Still other superintendents took some time off or decided to retire from superintendency altogether. The common thread among all of these superintendents was that they were able to achieve some control over the situation by exercising a variety of options for their next career steps.

After TG realized that the board's talk and actions were not consistent, he decided it was time to depart from the district. TG quietly but actively sought other positions outside of public education. He actually had obtained a new and better position six weeks before he officially resigned from the superintendency.

Another key lesson of good departure management was to leave the district as healthy as possible. Although there may have been resentment or other emotions directed at individuals directly responsible for the departure, no resentment toward the school district was voiced by any of the superintendents interviewed. This "big picture" view enabled all of the superintendents to maintain their roles as district stewards until the actual date of departure, and ultimately they wanted to see the district survive and thrive through the transition. This stewardship included big picture items, such as leaving with as much personal and community goodwill toward the district as possible, and detail items, such as leaving the office and operational affairs in good order for the next district leader.

It is important to note that several superintendents tried to leave with goodwill even though such feelings were not reciprocated. Often, the good work that superintendents had done received no formal acknowledgment in the wake of the unanticipated departure. Several superintendents expressed deep hurt at the lack of personal recognition all while trying their best to leave the district in a position to survive and thrive for the next superintendent and beyond.

Many superintendents discussed the effects of the departure process on central office and building staff. Change in leadership creates a great deal of tension, unrest, and uncertainty among staff at all levels in the district, and superintendents understood the importance of being supportive and demonstrating their best leadership philosophies and principles during the departure process. Many superintendents indicated that they had a great deal of support among staff during the departure process, and keeping the work of student learning at the forefront of daily business was paramount to successfully managing an unanticipated departure.

Several superintendents expressed the importance of not becoming isolated. Staying involved with the district, making the day-to-day decisions that a superintendent is authorized and required to make, supporting staff, and being physically and emotionally present throughout the departure process is not only good for the well-being of the district, it is also personally healthy. The stress and negative attention that accompanies an unanticipated departure can lead to a tendency to isolate oneself from work and family, and many superintendents cautioned strongly against succumbing to this tendency.

There is no "right time" to seek emotional support or psychological help from a professional counselor, religious leader, spouse, close family member, or friend. Virtually all of the superintendents interviewed indicated that they needed some type of personal emotional support throughout the management phase of the departure, and it is this support that kept them grounded and able to make good decisions for both self and district. An overwhelming number of superintendents credited the things they did well during the departure process with having an emotional support system to work through the personal feelings associated with this often traumatic process.

The superintendent's position is a consuming one. Most superintendents stressed the importance of not letting the job define the person, especially during an unanticipated departure. It is critical to be a "whole" person outside of superintendency. Personal and academic interests, hobbies, skills, and relationships that define who a person is outside of the role of superintendent are critical to recognize and, to the extent possible, maintain throughout the unanticipated departure process.

Once the management phase has begun, it has been cognitively recognized that an unanticipated departure is probably imminent. Superintendents indicated that it was important to understand that at this point, the board cannot be changed. The time for trying to reason with the board or fix the issues and problems is past. The management phase of departure is a different journey. This phase is highlighted by the implementation of an exit strategy, and each individual's strategy will be different depending on the personalities and circumstances involved. Regardless, a purposeful yet flexible strategy is critical to negotiate the management phase successfully.

When negotiating the terms of the departure, most superintendents believed that it was important to make a clean break from the district. Many advocated strongly for leaving the community, even if roots had been established. In some instances, the superintendents were not welcome in the district in any capacity, which was reflected in their separation agreements.

An important point that superintendents identified is that they should be careful about over- or underestimating their importance or value in their positions as district leaders. When things get rocky, there can be a tendency to focus on oneself and on evaluating all of the things that an individual brings through experience and institutional history, and to either inflate or marginalize those things. Superintendents who overestimate their importance and worth and let these attitudes manifest themselves in behaviors may leave the district scarred and divided. This kind of damage can take years to repair.

Finally, it is critical for both board and superintendent to maintain professionalism and avoid allegations, personal blame, and attacks in public and private as much as possible throughout the departure process. An effective tool for controlling these allegations and attacks are nondisparagement clauses in separation agreements, which stipulate that both sides agree that they will not disparage the other in any way in the future. Although these nondisparagement clauses do not stop all negative media and district attention on the departure, they prevent those in the highest leadership positions (board and superintendent) from damaging the reputations of those on the other side.

Recovery and Reflection

Key Findings in the Recovery and Reflection Phase

- The recovery process can take some time, and pain can linger.
- When you leave, leave; do not follow district news and gossip.
- Maintain a strong personal support system after the departure.
- Realize that where you end up after the departure is likely to be a better fit for your skill sets, strengths, and interests.

Unanticipated departures are traumatic processes. They are hard on superintendents, boards, districts, families, and the community. Each individual or entity needs time to regain normalcy and move forward. The nature of the unanticipated departure, how it is managed, and individual characteristics typically determine what is needed for recovery and how long it may take. Some superintendents seem to move on fairly easily, while others carry hurt and a variety of negative emotions for many years.

> During a major construction project in CW's district, a board member decided that he wanted to oversee the project and set up an office across the hall from the superintendent in a small meeting room that was rarely used except for occasional small-group meetings. After completion of the construction project, the board member stayed and started to oversee other operations, effectively acting as a "boss" to the superintendent at central office. This arrangement led to a long and bitter period of growing animosity between the board and super-

intendent, which resulted in the superintendent being asked to leave before his contract was fulfilled. CW still harbors feeling of resentment and hurt over the high level of micromanaging, and the prolonged vote of "no confidence" that resulted in his early departure.

The superintendents interviewed had all given a great deal of thought and consideration to their unanticipated departures, and they all learned valuable lessons from the process. However, there was large variance in the amount of these lessons learned that they had shared with others. For many of the superintendents, the interviews for this project were the first time that they had talked about their experiences with anyone other than family, close friends, religious leaders, and/or professionals. Many superintendents commented with surprise regarding how much they had to say and realized anew the value in the lessons that the process had taught them. No one was at a loss for suggestions and advice, with each being able to clearly identify those strategies, techniques, and decisions that were most helpful to them.

Key Lessons around Recovery and Reflection

Many of the important lessons learned about the recovery and reflection phase were extensions of the lessons learned in the management phase. The most striking thing about the responses relating to recovery and reflection was an overall sense of moving on and optimism about the future for themselves, and a genuine hope that the districts that they served would continue to move forward and successfully serve the students, parents, staff, and community in which they were located. However, there was also an underlying acknowledgment that some of the pain of the experience still lingers and that it would still take some time to completely recover.

Superintendents were overall adamant that it was important to completely leave the district. Phrases like "when you leave, leave," "remove yourself from the situation as much as possible," and "it is best to move out of the community" were prevalent in the responses. They cautioned against lurking on blogs, reading too many papers, or talking "shop" with former employees. It is important for both personal and district recovery to create physical and emotional space with all concerned so that healing can occur.

Another lesson learned in the recovery and reflection process was the importance of having a strong support system, not only when problems arise but also when things are going well. Once the support system is in place, superintendents continued to cultivate that system and learned the importance of strong personal support from sources outside the district in a successful superintendency. For some, the departure process was the first time that they had put a formal support system in place, and these individuals discussed the ways in which those relationships have continued to enrich their lives in meaningful ways beyond the departure process.

Finally, several superintendents who took another position immediately or soon after the unintended departure found that the new position was a much better fit for them in ways that they did not realize until they were in the new position. These superintendents learned the value of working to personal strengths and becoming more candid with themselves and others about their skill sets. This enhanced self-awareness enabled these superintendents to use their strengths as a way to help them find positions where their service would be best utilized.

An unanticipated departure from a superintendent position is a very personal journey in a very public forum. Though sometimes painful, each superintendent experienced valuable growth, often both professionally and personally. Most of the superintendents are currently in positions in which they find value, satisfaction, and fulfillment. They are doing meaningful work, regardless of whether they continue on as superintendents, serve in some other role in education, serve in another field altogether, or have retired.

A DIFFERENT TYPE OF CONCLUSION

There is great value in all of the advice given by the superintendents we interviewed, and we are so very grateful to them for sharing their experiences with us. If you are reading this book, it is probably because you are preparing to become a superintendent or are already a superintendent, and you may or may not be at some stage of an unanticipated departure. The experience will change you, and we would not presume to predict how. However, we can offer the experiences of several others who have been through it and who were willing to share their wisdom and experiences.

Perspective is critical, no matter where you are in life or what you are doing.

Dr. John Thurston has written this unpublished, thought-provoking reflection entitled "Suggestions for 'Changelings,' Those People Who Want a Happier and More Effective Life." Dr. Thurston has a PhD in clinical psychology and taught for many years at the University of Wisconsin—Eau Claire (professor emeritus of psychology). At age eighty-five, he remains an active writer, philosopher, and communicator. Dr. Thurston offers a wonderful perspective that can be used to step back and reflect anytime when things start to get too heavy and overwhelming.

We believe Dr. Thurston's twenty suggestions will provide readers with a welcome, practical yet effective way to perhaps begin to process the information in this book and/or in your professional journeys, wherever they may take you. Dr. Thurston encourages readers to have a sense of humor and to consider the suggestions. We agree.

Superintendents who have experienced an unanticipated departure may find several of the twenty suggestions to have merit. Dr. Thurston thinks each of us can likely find merit in at least two or three of the suggestions. The time during an unanticipated departure is a natural one to do some deep soul-searching into the roots of career and life. We hope you enjoy the humor and advice of a wise man.

1. *Plan.* Identify important personal goals that one must accomplish during the next five years. Determine what one must do today and during the next few months in order to achieve these goals. Don't accept the easy rationalizations that one is too busy or that one will get one's true reward in heaven. And don't be unduly dismayed when your plans don't work out for you. You will find that such failures are virtually inevitable. Regroup and keep trying. There's enjoyment and hope in each contemplation and the need for revision. This clearly applies to your use of "The Twenty Suggestions."
2. *Travel.* A conditional suggestion, for one should travel only for one's own personal reasons. Exposure to different people and cultures can enable you to learn a lot—about them and yourself. While travel can be a rich and rewarding growth experience, some people travel often and widely only to impress other people. They return weary and unchanged because, in reality, they have never left home. Your "bluebird of happiness" may reside in your own backyard.
3. *Be kind to others and to oneself.* In addition to being generally kind and considerate to others, one should engage in special acts of generosity from time to time. While both the giver and the participant will profit from this activity, the giver may gain even more by remaining anonymous. It's equally important to do kindness unto one's self even when others have not seen fit to do that unto one.
4. *Spend.* Scrooge should be no one's patron saint. Once prudent plans have been made for immediate and eventual financial security, spend freely of one's time and money for one's own enjoyment and that of others. Admirable charities such as food banks are available. Any ultimate measure of one's worth will probably make no sense to one's accountant. Spend yourself. Use some of your time and energy in the service of others who may be less fortunate. You'll be richly rewarded.
5. *Do not advise.* A conditional suggestion in that this does not preclude free and generous provision of one's wisdom *upon request*. If asked, one must be properly humble and circumspect in the offering of one's advice and counsel.

6. *Do not accept advice.* A conditional suggestion that stresses self-reliance and a disdain for allowing others to assume responsibility for one's life. Dr. Phil, his merry band of experts, and others of his mindset glibly provide at best only tools and a bit of motivation. In real life, only the very rich could afford the professional services that Phil et al. prescribe. There is little, if any, verifiable evidence of the successes they report. However, *critical* consideration of advice or adverse opinion from others is acceptable. You must supply the "hard lifting" required of any improvement.
7. *Be genteel.* In increasingly uncivil times, it's to one's personal advantage to behave civilly. If you receive e-mail, "snail" mail, or phone calls, it is both polite and obligatory that you respond immediately, if not sooner. Even modest mannerly behavior, politeness, and attention to the sensitivities of others will mark one as a truly exceptional individual. In the long run, such gentility will redound to one's advantage. "What goes around, *does* come around."
8. *Be kind and helpful to animals and birds.* One who harms animals/birds or extends dominion over them has his neighbor next on his hit list. It's a rare domestic animal that isn't thoroughly deserving of one's compassionate and unconditional love. The mere presence of a wild bird or animal in one's vicinity can cause one's spirits to soar. Seek out and cherish such experiences. Experience them fully.
9. *Engage in regular physical and mental exercises.* Do it! There are a host of indefensible reasons for procrastinating. Overriding obstacles is both necessary and gratifying. Fun, good health, growth, and relaxation are some of the rewards. Accept the challenge of "pushing the envelope" while moving ahead to actualize one's full physical and mental capabilities.
10. *Take risks.* A risk-free life provides only a mere existence. Let one's memories be full of risks taken and results realized rather than the comforts of hazards avoided. Don't succumb to the temptation to take any softer and easier ways. Dream your dreams—and then go about realizing them.
11. *Think.* In an age wherein "experts" and computers are said to provide all the answers one really needs, one must realize that the development of significant challenges and their resolution requires deep, personalized, and avant-garde thought. No one should ever allow anyone else to do one's thinking.
12. *Converse meaningfully and with civility.* In the course of this exercise, one should listen attentively and courteously. Go beyond the commonplace talk about the weather or sports. Risk revealing oneself to others even though they may be disinterested or disdainful. Practice that currently unfashionable, demanding, and rare art of listening. Oth-

ers will benefit from this expression of one's caring and concern. Personal rewards shall accrue to those who are able to listen with compassion and understanding. Gossipers revel in their prattle in the vacuum that is their lives.

13. *Do not be fearful of silence.* If one has nothing to say, one should feel free to lapse into companionable silence. Some fear silence as though it were the plague. They waste precious moments in idle chatter or loud, empty, self-serving trumpeting that would drown out the braying of other asses. Silence can be truly "golden." The time saved can be utilized in thought and quiet contemplation.

14. *Honor the past and learn from it.* One should look to the future while realizing the importance of the past as a necessary prologue to it. One who ignores the lessons of personal history may be doomed to repeat mistakes. But it is clearly counterproductive to remain mired in the past, considering endlessly what one might or should have done. Similarly, don't waste time making extensive plans for an unpredictable future. It has been said "If you want to hear your God laugh uncontrollably, you have only to tell Him or Her your plans for the next five years."

15. *Do not perseverate.* Persevere but do not perseverate. Keep trying in the face of obstacles and failure but only up to a point. Decide when your efforts are merely perseverative, like hitting one's head repeatedly and unproductively against a wall. If you have been doing that, a change in tactics becomes mandatory. Acceptance of losses and abandoning a losing situation are parts of a winning strategy. "Woulda, coulda, shoulda" rumination is pointless. One excellent definition of "insanity" indicates that one is "insane" if he (or she) keeps doing the same thing over and over again with the expectation each time that the results will be different and better.

16. *Accept one's lot.* Dwelling on past and current mistakes will unnecessarily constrict, complicate, and diminish one's life. Learn from your mistakes. After accepting one's shortfall, move ahead. As Kierkegaard once said, we understand our lives backward but must live them forward.

17. *Exalt creativity, art, individuality, and one's special passions.* If one is creative, this gift should be flaunted and realized fully. If this talent is not in one's nature, it should be supported fully in others. One must exult in marching to the beat of one's own very unique and distant drum. It's good to dream about one's self and circumstance. To live fully, one must develop a special personal passion for some activity or involvement and then pursue it to the max. It should be so important that you will cry if you encounter serious problems along the way.

18. *Cultivate personal relationships.* One must be highly selective in choosing and investing in the important people in one's life. After that, the effort involving acceptance and tolerance may lead to truly important, deep, and rewarding personal relationships with those selected. Such a mind-set may counteract a developing trend, which makes such relationships rare and even unattainable.
19. *Do not "should" unto others.* Abandon the common practice of telling others what they "should" do. No one has the knowledge or authority necessary to dictate the conduct of another's life.
20. *Do not allow others to "should" unto one.* One is far better off being a hammer than a nail. One must remain an individual who is free from any domination by others, i.e., having people tell one what he or she should do. One is fully responsible for the conduct of one's life. That one is you! You should exult in your freedom and independence. Sing out your song loudly, proudly, and prolongedly.

Appendix 1

Name
Address 1
City, State, ZIP Code

Date

Dear:

This letter is being sent to you from Dr. Thomas F. Evert, a former Wisconsin superintendent, and Amy E. Van Deuren, a former school board member and current doctoral student in educational leadership (résumés enclosed). We are interested in researching how superintendents go through challenging transitions and exits from a school district (resigning or retiring from a superintendency) and how they move forward with their professional and personal lives. We would like to use the material we obtain through our research to write a book on the topic, and Ms. Van Deuren would also like to use the material as part of the data for a doctoral dissertation on the topic of school board training and professional development. We are requesting an opportunity to interview you for inclusion in the book and possibly the dissertation.

Several books and articles have addressed the circumstances that resulted in the superintendent leaving the district earlier than planned. All of the books and many of the articles focus on the difficulties and hardships of the experience. While we do not want to marginalize negative aspects of the departure experience, our work will focus on critical junctures: when you knew it was time to move on, when you actually left, how you left, and what role(s) the board, the community, the staff, and other stakeholders played in the events that resulted in your departure. We are also interested in exploring issues related to the "phases" often associated with the superintendency: Was there a "honeymoon" phase? What were the key phases and periods in your tenure? Were there issues with personnel and/or board transitions? In summary, we are interested in knowing whether there are patterns in the departure process and the subsequent adjustment process of superintendents who leave under less-than-ideal conditions.

Each story of departure is unique, whether or not it occurred as planned. We are interested in capturing these stories and looking for common threads or themes that may provide valuable insight to other superintendents. We are all aware that statistically superintendents do not enjoy long tenures in school districts. We believe that compiling the experiences of several superintendents will raise awareness for all superintendents (whether aspiring, current, retired, or out of the field) so that they are better equipped to handle the departure process, however it may occur, and can transition more smoothly to whatever comes next.

We plan to interview 20 to 50 current and retired superintendents on the topic of superintendent departure. Interviews can be conducted either in person or by phone, although an in-person interview is preferred. We will be happy to meet with you at the time and location of your choice. The interview process should take approximately 1.5 to 2 hours. We plan on recording your interview and will request written permission to use the material from this interview in both the book and dissertation projects. We will maintain your confidentiality by using pseudonyms and omitting identifiers such as location, school district name, landmarks, etc. Depending on where the interview takes us, we may wish to contact you for some follow-up as our work continues.

We will contact you by phone within the next two weeks to discuss the project further. In the meantime, please do not hesitate to contact us with any questions or concerns you may have. Your participation in this important work will play a key role in adding to the knowledge base regarding the challenges of the superintendency and the realities of the departure process. We view this project as an opportunity to give back to the profession and to make it stronger and more viable for future, current, and past.

Thank you for your time and consideration,

Thomas F. Evert, PhD

Amy E. Van Deuren, EdD

Appendix 2

SUPERINTENDENT INTERVIEWS

Subject Name:_____

Date:_____

E-mail/Phone:_____

Address:_____

A. INTRODUCTION

We are researching the short-term and long-term experiences superintendents have when they leave a position under less-than-ideal or unanticipated conditions. Your responses, which will be used anonymously along with the responses of approximately twenty other superintendents, will help us identify commonalities and differences of experience among those individuals who undergo an unanticipated departure process. In addition, we hope to identify techniques and strategies that have helped superintendents survive and thrive during and after such a departure. It is our hope that the information we obtain through these interviews can be helpful to other superintendents as they negotiate contracts, conduct daily operations, and undergo the departure process. Thank you for your time and willingness to participate in these interviews.

Appendix 2

B. DEMOGRAPHICS

1. Gender
2. Highest degree status
   Master's:_____
   Doctorate:_____
3. States in which you hold/have held a superintendent's license:_____
4. Total years experience in education
   11–20 years_____
   21–30 years_____
   30+ years_____
5. Total years of experience as superintendent
   1–5 years _____
   6–10 years_____
   11–15 years_____
   16–20 years_____
   20+ years_____
6. Number of superintendencies
   1 - _____
   2 - _____
   3 - _____
   4 - _____
   5 - _____
7. Type of district(s) in which you have served as superintendent:
   Rural_____
   Suburban_____
   Urban_____
8. Type of district in which you served the superintendency that is the subject of this interview:
   Rural_____
   Suburban_____
   Urban_____
9. Size of district in which you served the superintendency that is the subject of this interview:
   Small (1,000 or less students)_____
   Medium (1,000–5,000 students)_____
   Large (5,000-plus students)_____

C. QUANTITATIVE QUESTIONS—BACKGROUND ON DEPARTURE

1. How did you leave the superintendency that is the subject of this interview?
   Resigned_____
   Fired_____
   Retired_____
   Nonrenewed_____
   Other_____
2. Was there specific contract language that supported your departure?
3. During any time during your departure process, did you consult or retain the services of an attorney?
4. What were the contract conditions—financial and others—of your departure?

QUALITATIVE QUESTIONS—PERSONAL REFLECTION ON DEPARTURE

1. Describe the context in which you became the superintendent of this particular school district.
2. Describe the situation and factors that led to your departure of your superintendency. Did you see this coming? When did you know it was time to go and did you have an exit strategy?
3. Explain what your (a) immediate response and (b) long-term personal reactions were to the departure.
4. What was the board's role in your departure? Was the board acting in a unified manner?
5. Explain what effect the departure had on the school district.
6. Explain the effects the crisis had on your (a) family and (b) friends.
7. What strategy/strategies did you use to manage your departure?
8. What did you do to try to thrive after the departure?
9. What advice would you give to aspiring and/or current superintendents regarding such departures?
10. Based on what you believe in hindsight, would you have left earlier or differently? If yes, how, and why?
11. What exit strategies would you recommend based on your experiences?
12. How were you replaced?
13. What else would you like to say?

Thank you again for your time and insights. Would you like a copy of our completed research?

Appendix 3

I. Determine Your Attitude

    a. Be very proud of work and accomplishments.
    b. Don't tolerate negative stuff from the board; don't put up with it.
    c. Don't take your board for granted.
    d. Plan to leave from day one of your new job.
    e. Plan for WHEN, not IF you leave.
    f. Have confidence in yourself and understand the way the game is played. You will have conflict with board members, and you can't be afraid to be political.
    g. Try not to take it personally; leave with as many good feelings as you can.
    h. Don't feel secure in your job.
    i. Try not to personalize.
    j. Never take the board/superintendent relationship for granted.
    k. Take the high road.
    l. Be humble.
    m. Don't assume longevity.
    n. Be happy regardless—don't let the job define you.
    o. Avoid the "road of despair."
    p. Anticipate a flood of emotions at some point.

II. Considerations before Taking a Job

    a. Study a district in depth before taking a job there.
    b. Carefully assess the situation before you take the job.
    c. Consider setting contract renewal dates early (December).
    d. Be realistic about what you can and cannot do when hired.

      e. Hire an attorney to review contract and advise on other legal considerations.
      f. Really check it out—you must trust the new board.

III. Specific Guidelines and Issues Related to Departure
      a. Get out quick—try to find another position before you leave.
      b. Use all resources to help yourself.
      c. Don't let them drive you out.
      d. Leave with class.
      e. Get legal advice—don't be nice.
      f. Get back on the horse right away . . . I did, and it worked.
      g. Will be told to "get back on the horse"—may not be good advice.
      h. Let the break happen and move on.
      i. Communicate with your board.
      j. When you leave—leave.
      k. Look for a new job early.
      l. Superintendent shouldn't be the issue.
      m. Don't go back to the district.
      n. Don't become involved in picking your successor.
      o. Hold closed session—clear air, have evaluation.
      p. Ask "Do I have votes for my contract with the board?"
      q. Community support may appear to be there—likely it is not.
      r. Take advantage of your skills when leaving.

IV. Assessing and Reassessing Reality and Relationships
      a. Adults have trouble with change—acknowledge this!
      b. You can't change the board.
      c. You can stay too long in one place.
      d. Board must support superintendent emotionally.
      e. Avoid becoming trapped as a savior.
      f. Know your values.
      g. Be honest with yourself.
      h. Understand—when asked to leave, you are not wanted.
      i. Anticipate the effect of new board members, try to learn their agendas.
      j. Be aware of the effects of a single issue.
      k. Deciding whether to leave or fight can be a difficult call.
      l. If you are considering a career change (getting into business), get on the right boards and be active politically.
      m. Keep lines of communication open with colleagues.
      n. Plan to leave from day one of your new job.
      o. Don't believe things are as they seem.

p. Realize you may not be the best match for your board.
q. School districts are inherently oppositional.
r. The superintendency is a political job; it may not be for you.
s. Short-term tenures are common in the superintendency.
t. Realize the transitional nature of the job.
u. Stay alert to signs that things have changed.
v. Recognize that change is part of the profession.
w. Realize it CAN happen to you.
x. Be clear in your motivation to be a superintendent, to "lead and serve."

V. Personal/Health Considerations

a. Health is #1; if stressed, then leave.
b. Realize your best friend is your spouse.
c. Rely on your support system.
d. Have physical activity; work out.
e. Cultivate friends in the district.
f. Try to keep emotions out of it.
g. Get psychological help when crisis hits.
h. Don't isolate yourself.
i. Have a personal and spiritual life.
j. Have outside interests; this is not life or death most of the time.
k. Rely on your family and friends; have outside interests.
l. Family is important.
m. Find a caring person outside the district for support during departure.

VI. Legal/Professional Issues

a. Leave your office orderly with everything intact.
b. Work with your school attorney.
c. Know that schools will be okay when you are gone—be reassured.
d. Get legal advice—don't be nice.
e. Become a resource to other superintendents.
f. Use any superintendent experience to get a new job.
g. Discuss what's going on with the board.
h. Talk to your board.

VII. Succession Planning

a. Try to mentor younger administrator and set stage for their growth.
b. Create a support system.
c. Be prepared to leave the superintendent job for another position.

References

Ackerman, R. H., & Maslin-Ostrowski, P. (2002). *The Wounded Leader: How Real Leadership Emerges in Times of Crisis.* San Francisco: Jossey-Bass.

Allison, E. (2012). "The resilient leader." *Educational Leadership, 69*(4), 79–82.

Badaracco Jr., J. L. (2002). *Leading Quietly.* Boston: Harvard Business Press.

Borba, A. L. (2010)."The superintendent's evaluation: Bridging the gap from theory to practice." http://www.aasa.org/content.aspx?id=12766.

Byrd, J., Drews, C., & Johnson, J. (2006). "Factors impacting superintendent turnover: Lessons from the field." *Education Leadership Review, 7*(2), 11 pages.

Cambron-McCabe, N., Cunningham, L. L., Harvey, J., & Koff, R. H. (2005). *The Superintendent's Field Book.* Thousand Oaks, CA: Corwin.

Cooper, B. S., Fusarelli, L. D., & Carella, V. A. (2000). "Career crisis in the school superintendency: The results of a national survey." Washington, DC: AASA National Center for Education Statistics, pp. 2–51.

Domenech, D. (Sept. 2011). Keynote address to the Wisconsin Association of School District Administrators, fall conference, Madison, WI.

DuFour, R. (2007). "In praise of top-down leadership." *School Administrator, 64*, 38–42.

Eadie, D. (2002). *Five Habits of High-Impact School Boards.* Lanham, MD: Scarecrow Education.

Eadie, D. (2003). *Eight Keys to an Extraordinary Board–Superintendent Partnership.* Lanham, MD: Scarecrow Education.

Eadie, D. (2009). "Boards and superintendents: A precious but fragile bond." *Illinois Association of School Boards.* http://www.iasb.com/journal/j030409_04.cfm.

Eadie, D. (2012). "Healthy relationships." *American School Board Journal, 199*(3), 38–39.

Federal Emergency Management Agency (FEMA). (2012)."The four phases of emergency management training." www.fema.gov/emiweb/downloads/is10_unit3.doc.

Fusarelli, B. C. (2006). "School board and superintendent relations: Issues of continuity, conflict, and community." *Journal of Cases in Educational Leadership, 9*(1), 44–57.

Gladwell, M. (2008). *Outliers.* New York: Little, Brown.

Hargreaves, A. (2009). "Leadership succession and sustainable improvement." *School Administrator, 66,* 10–14.

Hoyle, J. R., Bjork, L. G., Collier, V., & Glass, T. (2005). *The Superintendent as CEO: Standards-Based Performance.* Thousand Oaks, CA: Corwin, American Association of School Administrators.

Kamler, E. (2011). "Decade of difference: 1995–2005." *Educational Administration Quarterly, 45*(1), 115–44.

Kersten, T. A. (2010). *Stepping into Administration: How to Succeed in Making the Move.* Lanham, MD: Rowman & Littlefield.

Keane, W. G., & Moore, D. (2001). "The disappearing superintendent applicant: The invitation to apply goes unanswered." In C. C. Brunner & L. Bjork (Eds.), *The New Superintendency: Advances in Research and Theories of School Management and Educational Policy,* Vol. 6. Kidlington, UK: Elsevier Science.

Kinsella, M. P. (2004). "A school district's search for a new superintendent." *Journal of School Leadership, 14,* 286–307.

Kowalski, T. J., McCord, R. S., Peterson, G. J., Young, I. P., & Ellerson, N. (2011). *The American School Superintenendent: 2010 Decennial Study.* Lanham, MD: Rowman & Littlefield.

Lunenburg, F. C., & Ornstein, A. C. (2012). *Educational Administration: Concepts and Practices,* 6th ed. Belmont, CA: Wadsworth.

Marzano, R. J., Waters, T., & McNulty, B. (2009). *District Leadership That Works: Striking the Right Balance.* Bloomington, IN: Solution Tree Press.

Mathews, J., Floyd, D. G., Ilg, T., & Rohn, C. A. (2002). "Succession: Insiders vs. outsiders." *School Administrator, 59*(5). http://0proquest.umi.com.oscar.edgewood.edu/.

McAdams, D. (2012). "Engaging your board in reform policy work." *School Administrators, 2*(69), 12.

McAdams, R. (1997). "A systems approach to school reform." *Phi Delta Kappa, 79*(2), 138–43.

McCarthy, R. J., & Bennett, J. H. (1991). "If you're fired, here's how to land on your feet." *Executive Educator,* April, 14–17.

Namit, C. (2008). "Sharpening a district leadership model." *District Adminstration, 44,* 54–59.

Odden, A., & Picus, L. (2007). *School Finance: A Policy Perspective.* New York: McGraw-Hill.

Pascopella, A. (2011). "Superintendent staying power." *District Administration, 47*(4), 31–40.

Patterson, J. (2000). *The Anguish of Leadership.* Arlington, VA: American Association of School Adminisrators.

Patterson, J., & Kelleher, P. (2005). *Resilient School Leaders: Strategies for Turning Adversity into Achievement.* Arlington, VA: American Association of School Administrators.

Polka, W. S., & Litchka, P. R. (2008). *The Dark Side of Educational Leadership: Superintendents and the Professional Victim Syndrome.* Lanham, MD: Rowman & Littlefield Education.

Reeves, R. (2006). *What Every Rookie Superintendent Should Know.* Lanham, MD: Rowman & Littlefield.

Samuel, C. (2011). "Survey detects shifting priorities of school boards." *Education Week, 30*(20), February 9, 22.

Sternberg, R. (2001). "The ultimate stress." *School Administrator, 58,* xx.

Stover, D. (2011). "Walking the line." *American School Board Journal, 198*(2), 17–20.

Sutton, C. M., & Job, M. P. (2008). *2007 State of the Superintendent Mini-Survey: A spring to the Superintendency.* Arlington, VA: American Association of School Administrators.

Thurston, J. R. (n.d.). *Suggestions for Changelings, Those People Who Want a Happier and More Effective Life.* Unpublished manuscript.

Underwood, J., & Mead, J. F. (2012). "A smart ALEC threatens public education." *Phi Delta Kappan, 93*(6), 51–55.

Vasudeva, A. (2009). "Training for succession." *School Administrator, 66,* 16–19.

About the Authors

Thomas F. Evert, PhD, is a former public school superintendent of fourteen years and served as a high school principal and director of student services. Evert is currently serving as a doctoral dissertation liaison and teaches doctoral courses in law, media, curriculum, and instruction at Edgewood College.

Amy E. Van Deuren, EdD, is assistant professor at National Louis University and serves as the Program Coordinator for Educational Leadership at the Milwaukee, Wisconsin, campus. She teaches graduate courses in school law, school-community relations, student-centered schools, finance, policy, and research. Van Deuren has coauthored several books in the fields of educational leadership and music education.

www.ingramcontent.com/pod-product-compliance
Lightning Source LLC
Chambersburg PA
CBHW052132300426
44116CB00010B/1875